UNIX in Plain English

Second Edition

Kevin Reichard

and Eric Foster-Johnson

MIS:
PRESS

Henry Holt & Co., • New York

MIS:Press
A Subsidiary of Henry Holt and Company, Inc.
115 West 18th Street
New York, New York 10011
http://www.mispress.com

Limits of Liability and Disclaimer of Warranty

The Author and Publisher of this book have used their best efforts in preparing the book and the programs contained in it. These efforts include the development, research, and testing of the theories and programs to determine their effectiveness.

The Author and Publisher make no warranty of any kind, expressed or implied, with regard to these programs or the documentation contained in this book. The Author and Publisher shall not be liable in any event for incidental or consequential damages in connection with, or arising out of, the furnishing, performance, or use of these programs.

All products, names and services are trademarks or registered trademarks of their respective companies.

Second Edition—1997

Library of Congress Cataloging-in-Publication Data

Reichard, Kevin
  UNIX in Plain English / Kevin Reichard, Eric F. Johnson. -- 2nd Ed.
    p.   cm.
  Includes Index
  ISBN 1-55828-549-0
  1. UNIX (Computer file) 2.Operating systems—(computers)
  I. Johnson, Eric F. II. Title.
  QA76.76063R4448   1997
  005.4'32--dc21
                                                        97-19174
                                                           CIP

MIS:Press and M&T Books are available at special discounts for bulk purchases for sales promotions, premiums, and fundraising. Special editions or book excerpts can also be created to specification.

For details contact: Special Sales Director
                              MIS:Press and M&T Books
                              Subsidiaries of Henry Holt and Company, Inc.
                              115 West 18th Street
                              New York, New York 10011

10 9 8 7 6 5 4 3 2 1

Associate Publisher: *Paul Farrell*   **Production Editor:** *Stephanie Doyle*
Executive Editor: *Shari Chappell*   **Copy Edit Manager:** *Karen Tongish*
Editor: *Laura Lewin*   **Copy Editor:** *Annette Devlin*

Contents

Chapter 1
UNIX Overview: Commands
and Structures 7

Chapter 2
UNIX in Plain English 17

Chapter 3
UNIX/DOS Cross Reference 27

Chapter 4
UNIX Commands A to Z 33

Chapter 5
UNIX Commands, Organized
by Group 41

Chapter 6
System-Administration
Commands 375

Chapter 7
Shell Commands
and Variables 391

Chapter 8
FTP Commands 405

Chapter 9
Window Managers 411

Bibliography 425

Index 429

Introduction

Welcome to *UNIX in Plain English!* This reference work is designed to give you instant access to the UNIX and X Window System commands and concepts you'll use in your everyday work. In many ways, we merely organized the many handwritten notes sitting next to our terminals and the Post-It notes attached to our monitors in a fashion that benefits both beginning and advanced UNIX users. We, too, tired of flipping through disorganized notes and reference books that end up being more complex than the documentation.

Why do you need a reference work like this, when you have manuals upon manuals lining your bookshelves in addition to an online help system?

To be honest, finding information on UNIX systems is an onerous chore. UNIX documentation tends to be on the weak side when it comes to looking up anything quickly: The manuals provide a wealth of advanced technical information, but they assume a certain level of familiarity with computing in general and the UNIX operating in particular. Yes, most UNIX systems have online manual (**man**) pages that cover the entire command set. But in order to use the manual page, you first need to know the name of the command. Because most of us don't know exactly what we want until we find it—the best argument, incidentally, for extensive hypertext help systems—in many ways, the online man pages aren't much help. Plus, UNIX is definitely geared for the educated user. Once

1

you understand the basic mechanisms, commands, and structures, you'll do reasonably well in your everyday work,and the basics, you're in trouble.

That's where the second edition of *UNIX in Plain English* comes in. We've assembled lists of the UNIX and X Window command sets in alphabetical order, by type, and cross-referenced with DOS commands. We've also added a section that lists the computer task and then offers the necessary UNIX command, working backwards from the usual reference format.

This book is also designed as a companion to *Teach Yourself UNIX*, third edition (MIS:Press, 1996). We wrote *Teach Yourself UNIX* purely as a beginners' tutorial, although we did include a reference section. *UNIX in Plain English* is meant as an extension of that reference section. We hope that you'll take the time to look up the extended explanations of important commands in *Teach Yourself UNIX*. While we list all of the command-line options for all UNIX commands in this work, you can find fuller explanations in *Teach Yourself UNIX* for the major UNIX commands. If you're looking for more information about some of the lesser-known UNIX commands, you can either rush out and buy yet *another* UNIX text (we list some essential works in the Bibliography) or check your system documentation.

How This Book Is Organized

We find that our searches for information on UNIX commands are accomplished several different ways:

- We know exactly what we're looking for, and all we need is the information about a specific command. (As you might expect, this option occurs least often.)

- We're not quite sure what we're looking for, but we know exactly what we want to do. (Another unlikely occurrence because we rarely know exactly what we want to do.)

- We have a vague idea of what we want to do. (This occurs more frequently in real life than in computing.)

- We're not quite sure what we want to do, but we know it's similar to something that we know how to do.

- We're totally lost and want to browse through our options. (Bingo!)

That's why we've decided to organize UNIX and X Window commands in several different ways. Most UNIX/X reference works list all the commands in alphabetical order, based on the assumption that you know exactly what you're looking for and therefore can look it up in an mondo listing of commands. (Yeah, right.) While we included an alphabetical listing of the commands we cover in this book (Chapter 4, "UNIX from A to Z"), we've also included several other sections that present UNIX commands in slightly different formats. Chapter 2, "UNIX in Plain English," presents a whole slew of common computing tasks, along with the corresponding UNIX and/or X command. For DOS users, we've organized a list of all DOS commands (Chapter 3, "UNIX/DOS Cross Reference") and their counterparts in UNIX. Finally, the heart of the book—Chapter 5, "UNIX Commands, Organized by Group"—divides UNIX commands into broad categories (printing, text processing, and so on).

This section also tells you where you can find the extended explanation of the command. We've organized these explanations into what we feel is an easy-to-use format: The commands are displayed in large type at the top of the page, followed by sections on usage, examples, options, arguments, related commands, and any other relevant information. We've purposely left a lot of space around these command listings; if you're like us, you'll soon be making notes for yourself in the margins.

Differences Between the First and Second Editions

We augmented the best-selling first edition with more than 80 new commands, including an expanded list of programming commands and totally new coverage of X Window System commands. When we wrote the first edition, we decided not to include X commands because we found that it hadn't yet gained wide acceptance among UNIX users.

However, the UNIX world has evolved to the point where X is fairly ubiquitous. In this edition, we added X Window commands as well as common commands from the Common Desktop Environment (CDE) suite of tools.

Conventions Used in This Book

All commands can be found in **boldface** throughout the book. Commands that are to be typed directly into the system are displayed in a `monospaced` typeface.

In addition, you should be aware of some of the references still used in the UNIX operating system:

- **Bell**. Back in the old days of teletype data entry, the machines featured a bell, much like the typewriters of that era. Because there was often little feedback between a user and the computer, the computer would ring a bell to attract the attention of the user, who more than likely was across the room staring out the window. Today, of course, computers don't have bells, they have speakers. A reference to a *bell* usually means a beep emanating from the speaker.

- **Case**. In UNIX, the case matters when you're dealing with files. For instance, **Kevin.report** is different from **kevin.report** and **kevin.Report** and **Kevin.Report**.

- **Keys**. Not every UNIX keyboard features the same set of keys. In fact, keyboards differ quite a bit, as

4

vendors like Sun Microsystems, Hewlett-Packard, DEC, and IBM introduce variations on the standard keyboard. For the purposes of this book, we're not going to get into a discussion of differing keyboards, and for the most part the keys mentioned within this book should be present on all keyboards. However, there are two things you should note: The **Enter** and the **Return** keys are the same (in this book, we'll use **Enter** because that seems to be the trend in modern UNIX usage), while the backspace key is usually labeled **Backspace**, **BkSp**, or ←.

A Word of Warning

Even though this is a comprehensive reference work about the UNIX operating system, you should be aware that we have not included every single option for every single command. In fact, we're not even listing every single command. To be honest, there are many obscure UNIX commands that you're never going to even come close to using, and some UNIX commands have been superseded by newer, more effective commands.

Why not list these commands? Because this book was written with the KISS principle in mind: Keep It Simple, Stupid. We've focused on the commands that most beginning and intermediate UNIX users would need access to most of the time.

Therefore, we're not covering commands like **ar** (archive), because it's highly unlikely that the vast majority of UNIX users will ever need it—it's also highly unlikely that they'll notice its absence.

UNIX Variants

A book like this must confront the inevitable issue of how much of the UNIX operating system to cover and which UNIX variants to cover.

Throughout much of its history, UNIX was developed by a group within AT&T (which AT&T later sold to Novell). Other early UNIX work was done at the University of California at Berkeley, which lead to BSD UNIX (Berkeley Software Distribution). Most major UNIX vendors took what they thought was the best of the AT&T UNIX, mixed in BSD features, and added their own extensions to the pot, resulting in many similar, but slightly different, versions of UNIX.

Currently UNIX is a veritable Tower of Babel, with differing versions from Sun Microsystems (SunOS, Solaris), Hewlett-Packard (HP-UX), IBM (AIX), SCO (SCO UNIX), as well as various Intel-based versions (BSD, Linux).

While vendors are working to eliminate many of these differences, don't be surprised if your system doesn't support all the commands and all the options listed in this book. We've tried to flag the most obvious instances of commands and options that are not found on every system. We tested the commands and options in this book on several systems, but as in life, nothing is guaranteed.

One UNIX workalike we purposely avoided was Linux, the freely available tool for PCs. A separate MIS:Press title, *Linux in Plain English*, covers the Linux command set (see the Bibliography for details).

How to Reach the Authors

We welcome your feedback. You can reach us via electronic mail at reichard@mr.net. If you prefer more mundane means of communication, you can drop us a line in care of the publisher.

1

UNIX Overview: Commands and Structures

On the surface, UNIX appears to be an unnecessarily complex operating system—just witness the large number of commands listed later in this book. But underneath the surface lie the roots of a very simple and elegant operating system. The details may be complex, but the mechanisms tend toward the simple.

A good example is the mechanism for telling the computer exactly what you want to do. If you weren't familiar with UNIX, you might be intimidated by this cryptic symbol on the screen:

```
$
```

This is called a **prompt**, and it lets you know that the system is waiting for you to enter a command. Of course, if you didn't have any background in UNIX, you'd be quite confused at this point. But once you learn that the $ symbol is a prompt and that it indicates that the system is waiting for a command from you, the all-powerful user, then UNIX isn't quite so intimidating. (There are several symbols used to denote a prompt, depending on which shell you're using. The Korn and Bourne shells use $ as the prompt; the C shell uses %. But we're getting ahead of ourselves here. At this point, just note the existence of a prompt; also remember that when we use a prompt with an example, you are *not* to type in the prompt symbol when you enter a command line.)

Commands

The sense of enlightenment is furthered when you first learn how to interact with the computer. Remember at all times: *The computer is not smarter than you are.* As a matter of fact, it's a lot dumber. Without instructions—called **commands**—from you, the computer can do little more than sit there and run up an electrical bill. It does exactly as you instruct. The key is making sure that what you instruct is what you want done.

With that in mind, you can confidently stride up to your terminal and enter a command. At the prompt, you enter a command (or multiple commands) as well as any arguments and options; the combination is called a **command line** or **command prompt**. Everything in UNIX is a command, no matter what you're trying to do. To run a program, you actually issue a command. To list the files in a directory, you issue a command. To run a text editor, you run a command.

As you know if you've peeked ahead, UNIX features literally hundreds of commands. Some of the commands are used frequently; for instance, text editors like **vi** or **ed** are very handy for creating short files or memos. Some commands are specific to certain versions of UNIX, while others can be found in virtually every UNIX variant. This book focuses on the commands that can be found almost everywhere. A typical command line looks something like this:

```
$ ls -1
```

The **-1** (one, not ell) in this command line is called an **option**. Options and arguments modify a command in some way, usually by narrowing the terms of the command. For instance, one of the many options associated with the **ls** command (which lists the contents—the files—of a directory) displays the output in a single column rather than the default of multiple columns. (As you've probably figured out, this refers to our command-line example in the previous paragraph.) There are *very* few commands that don't have any associated options, and mastering these options goes a long way toward simplifying your UNIX usage. (Chapter 5, which summarizes a majority of UNIX commands, stresses options in the Examples sections.)

When you run the above **ls** command line, your terminal will display something akin to the following:

```
$ ls -1
data
financials
personnel
misc
newdata
```

The actual filenames aren't important; for our discussion, the central point is that the files are listed in a single column. Without the **-1** option, the output from the **ls** command would look something like this:

```
$ ls
data        figures      newdata        personnel
misc        expenses     financials
```

This is a very minor example of an option. Most options have more far-reaching results, as you'll find out when you start using options in your daily UNIX usage.

Files

For the most part, commands aren't worth a whole lot if there isn't a **filename** involved. (There are a few exceptions, but those commands tend to be on the limited side, unless your UNIX usage is heavy on finding the current date and time with the **date** command.) Everything in UNIX is a file. And we mean *everything*. A directory is merely a file that represents a grouping of other files. A printer is represented by a file. A device, such as a tape drive, is represented by a file.

On one level, this makes things enormously simple: Commands work (mostly) on files. It's up to you to keep track of what the files represent, which makes things a tad more difficult.

A file is a computer structure used to store information in an electronic format that the computer can use: bits. A bit is either 0 or 1. When strung together, these bits comprise the characters we all recognize. A file is a method for organizing these bits in a logical format; otherwise, they'd be scattered around a hard disk with no reasonable method of retrieving them.

As mentioned, everything in UNIX is a file. When you run a text editor like **vi**, you're referencing a special file that executes a command. When you edit a file within **vi**, you're working with an ordinary text file. When you print that file with the **lp** command, you're sending it to a file representing a printer. And when you save the file in a subdirectory, you're really storing a reference to the file into a file representing the subdirectory.

Sound confusing? It can be, so don't worry too much about it. As time goes along and you work more with UNIX, you'll see how this all makes sense.

There are four types of files:

- Ordinary files
- Directories
- Special device files
- Links

There are subtypes within these types:

- **Ordinary files** can be text files (containing only ASCII characters), data files (for instance, a database file may contain characters other than ASCII characters), command text files (which provide commands to your system), and executable files (programs).

- **Directories** contain information about other files. We'll cover directories in more depth later in this chapter.

- **Special device files** are the files that control physical aspects of the computer system. For instance, when you use the **tar** command to create a tape archive, you're merely writing files to a file representing the tape drive (usually **/dev/rmt0**).

- **Links** allow the same file to be accessed under different names in different locations. Since UNIX is inherently a multiuser operating system, it makes more sense to preserve precious disk-space resources by creating links between the same file than to have each user keep a copy of the same file at his or her disposal.

Directories

Where there are files, there must be directories for organizing these files. Without directories, daily UNIX usage—particularly on a large installation where there may be hundreds of users—would be a nightmare as users tried to keep track of thousands and thousands of files, all lumped together.

As you saw in the previous section, a directory is nothing more than a file that references other files. A directory can be thought of as a file folder holding files and other directories (called **subdirectories**), which in turn can contain further files and additional directories. Every directory is actually a subdirectory of another directory, save one, which is designated by a slash (/). This is called the **root directory**.

This is why a filename *always* begins with a slash. A full filename indicates the position of a file within the directory tree. The top of the tree begins with the root directory (/), and that root directory holds other subdirectories (common directories at that level include **users**, **etc**, **usr**, and **tmp**). If you're working on a large system with a friendly system administrator, you've probably been assigned a **home directory**, which is

11

where you begin each UNIX session. This directory is probably contained somewhere as a subdirectory of the **users** subdirectory.

UNIX gives you many commands for creating, deleting, and managing directories. You'll probably want to create some directories of your own as you go along. The idea is to create directories that match your tasks; for instance, you may want to name a directory **reports** if it contains reports for your boss.

Dealing with directories can be confusing, especially when there are a lot of potential commands involved—this topic is beyond the scope of this reference work. See the Bibliography for a list of recommended books and tutorials on UNIX usage.

Standard Input/Output

Now that we know about files and commands, it's time to quickly explain how to use them.

More than one command can be issued at a time at the prompt. It's not uncommon to see a command prompt begin with a command and an option, followed by an instruction to send the output of that command to yet another command. In UNIXdom, this is called **standard input and output** (I/O) or **redirection**.

We'll illustrate this with a common UNIX command, **cat**. Running the **cat** command with no options looks like this:

```
$ cat
```

This merely allows you to enter keystrokes; when you hit the **Enter** key, your input will be repeated on the monitor. The keystrokes have not been saved to disk; once you display them on the screen, they're gone forever. Like most UNIX commands, **cat** assumes that standard input means input from the keyboard, and standard output means display on the terminal. (That's why the use of **cat** with no options or filenames merely displays your keystrokes on the terminal screen.) In this instance, **cat** is of little use, unless you enjoy having the computer mimic your keystrokes.

Cat becomes much more useful when a filename is used on the command line. To display the contents of an existing file onscreen, use **cat** along with the filename:

```
$ cat kevin.report
Because of declining sales, I recommend that
we halt production of the 1190-AAA widget
immediately.
```

In this case, we've countered **cat's** assumption that input will come from the keyboard by entering a filename. Therefore, **cat** displays the contents of the file to screen rather than your keystrokes.

With input/output commands, you can direct **cat** to perform many additional functions. For example, you may want to save your keystrokes to an ASCII file; in this instance, you'd use **cat** as an extremely limited text processor. The following command tells **cat** to send standard input—your keystrokes—to a file named **report.1997**:

```
$ cat > report.1997
```

In this instance, **cat** becomes a very rudimentary text editor. You enter text one line at a time; when you're done entering text, type **Ctrl-D** to end input. (Generally speaking, **Ctrl-D** will end input for the UNIX commands requiring input.)

You can also use **cat** as an alternate method for copying the contents of a file to a new file:

```
$ cat report.1998 > report.1998
```

This specifies both input (**report.1997**) and output (**report.1998**). The file report.1997 remains intact; the contents are copied into the new file **report.1998**. (By the way, this is how UNIX manages printing. A printer is set up as a file—remember, we warned you that everything in UNIX is a file of some sort. When you print a document, you direct the output of a command to a printer, as referenced by a file.)

Finally, you can append your keystrokes or an existing file to the end of another existing file:

```
$ cat report.1998 >> report.1997
```

Here you would be copying the contents of **report.1998** to the end of the file **report.1997**. If you want to add information directly to the end of the file **report.1997**, use the following:

```
$ cat >> report.1997
```

The above input/output commands are illustrated in Table 1.1:

Table 1.1 Input/Output Commands

SYMBOL	USAGE	RESULT
>	*command>filename*	Output of *command* is sent to *filename*.
<	*command<filename*	Input from *filename* is used by *command*.
>>	*command> filename*	Output of *command* is appended to *filename*.
|	*command1\command2*	Run *command1*, then send output to *command2*.

Smart readers will notice that the < symbol listed in Table 1.1 performs the equivalent of the following command, which we covered earlier:

```
$ cat kevin.report
```

This achieves the same result as:

```
$ cat < kevin.report
```

The difference lies in the manner in which the UNIX shell treats the two commands. In the first instance, the shell treats the filename, **kevin.report**, as an **argument** to the **cat** command. In the second instance, the shell treats **kevin.report** as input for the **cat** command.

You can use more than one input/output command in a single command line. For example, many UNIX commands—especially when working with shell scripts—look something like this:

```
$ command < infile > outfile
```

This tells the *command* to use input from *infile* and send the output to *outfile*.

Pipes

Standard input/output can be taken a step further when you introduce another powerful UNIX tool: **pipes**. A pipe is merely a method of sending the output of one command to be used as input for a second command. It looks like this:

```
$ command1 | command2
```

This is a **pipeline**. For instance, you may want to sort a file before printing it. In this case, you'd use the **sort** command to sort the file, and you'd send the output to the **lp** command to print the sorted file. (See Chapter 5 for more on the **sort** command.) The resulting command line looks something like this:

```
$ sort textfile | lp
```

You can enter multiple pipes on a command line; our example used one merely for illustrative purposes. Here's an example of a longer pipeline:

```
$ ls *.1994 | grep profits | lp
```

This command line searches for all files ending in **1994** in the current directory, then sends the output of that command to **grep**, which searches those files for the string *profits*. **Grep** then sends lines containing that string to the **lp** command, which prints out the lines.

2

UNIX in Plain English

Most of us know what we want to do when we sit down in front of a terminal. The challenge, then, is figuring out how to tell the operating system exactly what we want to do. Unfortunately, the operating system doesn't make it any easier; it's not very forgiving if your command doesn't quite match your goal.

This chapter is for those who know exactly what they want to do and need a lead on the corresponding UNIX command. We've listed common computing tasks in the left-hand column (the *italicized* keywords are in alphabetic order), and we've listed the conforming UNIX command in the right-hand column. Most commands are listed a few different ways; for instance, you can find the common **ls** command under both *list* and *file*.

append other files to an existing file	cat
track *appointments* and schedule meetings	cm, dtcm
create a tape *archive*	tar, cpio
search for *ASCII* strings within binary files	strings
search and replace *ASCII* characters	tr
create a tape *backup*	tar, cpio
print a 10-character *banner*	banner
start the *Bourne shell*	sh
start the *C shell*	csh
calculate your mortgage payments	calctool, dtcalc, xcalc
perform math *calculations*	bc, dc
display current month in *calendar* form	cal, cm, dtcm
display a *calendar*	cm, dtcm
call another terminal	ct
call another UNIX system	cu
cancel jobs scheduled with the **at** command	atrm
cancel print job	cancel
capture a screen image	xv, xwd
chat with another user on the network	talk
calculate a file's *checksum*	sum
clear the screen	clear
display a *column* from a sorted file	cut
strip *column*-formatting commands	col
combine presorted files with a common field	join
combine several files into a new file	cat
run *command* at specific time	at
enter UNIX *commands* in a graphical environment	xterm, dtterm, shelltool
run a series of *commands*	batch
time a *command*	time, timex
compare contents of two directories	dircmp

If you want to...	Use the UNIX command...
compare contents of two presorted files	**comm**
compare three files to see if they are different	**diff3**
compare two files and report on differing lines	**diff**
compare two files and return differing lines	**bdiff**
compare two files to see if they are different	**cmp**
compare two files and report differences and commonalities	**sdiff**
compile C programs	**cc**
compress a file	**compress, pack**
copy a file	**cat, cp, filemgr, dtfile**
copy files to and from networked remote systems	**rcp**
copy files to and from remote UNIX system	**uucp**
count the number of words in text file	**wc**
create a new text file	**cat, dtpad, textedit, xedit**
change *current directory*	**cd**
stop a *current process*	**kill**
display *date* and time	**date**
change a file's *date* to the current date	**touch**
decode file after communications	**uudecode**
delete a file	**rm, filemgr, dtfile**
create a *directory*	**mkdir, filemgr, dtfile**
display disk space used by a *directory*	**du**
generate a *directory* listing	**ls**
change current working *directory*	**cd**
remove a *directory*	**rmdir, filemgr, dtfile**
return current working *directory*	**pwd**
compare the contents of two *directories*	**dircmp**
display free or total *disk space*	**df**

UNIX in
Plain English

If you want to...	Use the UNIX command...
display *disk space* used by a directory	du
display a file	cat, page, dtpad, textedit, xedit
display a file one screen at a time	more
display first ten lines of a file	head
display last ten lines of a file	tail
display packed files	pcat
edit a text file	vi, ed, dtpad, textedit, xedit
send *electronic mail*	mailx, dtmail, mailtool
send return *electronic mail* when you're on vacation	vacation
notify you when *electronic mail* arrives	notify, xbiff
encode file before communications	uuencode
encrypt a file	crypt
display or set *environment variables*	env
format *equations*	eqn, neqn
erase a file	rm
exit	exit
copy a *file*	cat, cp, filemgr, dtfile
create a new text *file*	cat, dtpad, textedit, xedit
change a *file*'s date to the current date	touch
display a *file*	cat, page
display a *file* one screen at a time	more
display first ten lines of a *file*	head
display last ten lines of a *file*	tail
edit a *file*	vi, ed, dtpad, textedit, xedit
encrypt a *file*	crypt
erase a *file*	rm

If you want to...	Use the UNIX command...
find a *file*	**find**
format a structured *file*	**awk, nawk**
send output to *file* as well as to screen	**tee**
change ownership of *file*	**chown**
move a *file* or multiple files	**mv**
display a column from a sorted *file*	**cut**
sort a *file*	**sort**
sort a structured *file*	**awk, nawk**
search a structured *file*	**awk, nawk, grep**
split a *file* into smaller files	**csplit, split**
determine *file* type	**file**
change *file-access permissions*	**chmod**
create or determine default *file-access permissions*	**umask**
append other *files* to an existing file	**cat**
combine presorted *files* with a common field	**join**
combine several *files* into a new file	**cat**
compare contents of two presorted *files*	**comm**
compare three *files* to see if they are different	**diff3**
compare two *files* and report on differing lines	**diff**
compare two *files* and return differing lines	**bdiff**
compare two *files* to see if they are different	**cmp**
display packed *files*	**pcat**
merge *files* side by side	**paste**
change ownership of a group of *files*	**chgrp**
list *files*	**ls**
link *files*	**ln**
search for ASCII strings within binary *files*	**strings**
remove *files*	**rm**
find the *full filename*	**basename**
find a file	**find**
display a *font*	**xfd, xfontsel**

UNIX in Plain English

If you want to...	Use the UNIX command...
list available *fonts*	**xlsfonts, fsls fonts**
format equations	**eqn, neqn**
format images for laser printer	**xdpr, xpr**
format tables	**tbl**
format text file	**newform**
format a structured file	**awk, nawk**
format text for laser printer	**troff**
format text for line printer	**nroff**
format text (right justify)	**fmt**
format text to specific width	**fold**
enter UNIX commands in a *graphical environment*	**xterm, dtterm, shelltool**
log in new *group*	**newgrp**
find out what *groups* a user belongs to	**groups**
get *help*	**man, apropos, whatis, xman**
display user *ID*	**id**
capture a screen *image*	**xv, xwd**
display a screen *image*	**xv, xwud**
format *images* for laser printer	**xdpr, xpr**
start *Korn shell*	**ksh**
insert *line numbers* in text file	**nl**
link files	**ln**
list files	**ls**
save a *log* of your current computing session	**script**
log in as another user	**su**
log in new group	**newgrp**
log in remote system	**rlogin, telnet**
log in system	**login**
print your *login name*	**logname**
track *logins* to other remote systems	**uulog**

log off system	**exit**
run a command even after you *log off* the system	**nohup**
show who is *logged on* the system	**who, rwho**
run a command at a *low priority*	**nice**
send electronic *mail*	**mailx, dtmail, mailtool**
send return electronic *mail* when you're on vacation	**vacation**
notify you when *mail* arrives	**notify, check mail**
view *manual* pages	**man, xman**
perform *math* calculations	**bc, dc**
merge files side by side	**paste**
send *message* to all users logged on the system	**wall**
turn on/off the ability to receive *messages* from other users	**mesg**
calculate your *mortgage* payments	**calctool, dtcalc, xcalc**
move a file or multiple files	**mv**
display system *news*	**news**
show status of all machines on *network*	**ruptime**
run a command *nicely* (at a lower priority)	**nice**
send *output* to file as well as to screen	**tee**
change *ownership* of file	**chown**
change *ownership* of a group of files	**chgrp**
pack a file	**compress, pack**
display *packed* files	**pcat**
set your *password*	**passwd**
pause before executing a command	**sleep**
print	**lp, lpr, dtlp**
prepare a file for *printing*	**pr**
print a 10-character banner	**banner**
cancel *print* job	**cancel**

UNIX in
Plain English

If you want to...	Use the UNIX command...
print jobs scheduled with **at** command	atq
show status of *print* requests	lpstat
start *print spooler*	lpsched
stop *print spooler*	lpshut
stop a current *process*	kill
show current *processes*	ps
quit	exit
schedule *recurring* tasks	crontab
start a *remote shell* on a remote system	rsh
copy files to and from *remote system*	rcp, uucp, ftp
log on *remote system*	telnet, rlogin
start a remote shell on a *remote system*	rsh
run a UNIX command on a *remote system*	uux
track logins to other *remote systems*	uulog
remove a directory	rmdir, filemgr, dtfile
remove files	rm, filemgr, dtfile
run a UNIX command on a remote system	uux
schedule personal events	calendar, cm, dtcm
schedule recurring tasks	crontab
capture a *screen* image	xv, xwd
search a structured file	awk, nawk, grep
search for text string	egrep, grep, fgrep
search and replace ASCII characters	tr
sort a file	sort
sort a structured file	awk, nawk
check *spelling* in text file	spell
split a file into smaller files	csplit, split

If you want to...	Use the UNIX command...
display to *standard output*	**echo**
show *status* of all machines on the network	**ruptime**
search for text *string*	**egrep, grep, fgrep**
strip column-formatting commands	**col**
strip formatting commands	**deroff**
return UNIX *system name*	**uname**
display *system news*	**news**
list *systems* that you can communicate with	**uuname**
format *tables*	**tbl**
set *tabs*	**tabs**
create a *tape* backup	**tar, cpio**
display *terminal* information	**tput**
display *terminal* options	**tty**
set *terminal* configuration	**stty**
check spelling in *text* file	**spell**
edit *text* file	**vi, ed, dtpad, textedit, xedit**
format *text* file	**newform**
format *text* for laser printer	**troff**
format *text* for line printer	**nroff**
format *text* (right justify)	**fmt**
format *text* to specific width	**fold**
insert line numbers in *text* file	**nl**
create a new *text file*	**cat, dtpad, textedit, xedit**
search for *text string*	**egrep, grep, fgrep**
display date and *time*	**date**
run command at specific *time*	**at**
time a command	**time, timex**
determine file *type*	**file**

If you want to...	Use the UNIX command...
uncompress a file	**uncompress**
unpack a file	**unpack**
display *user ID*	**id**
list *users*	**listusers**
display information about other *users* on the system	**who**
find information about other *users* on the system	**finger**
show status of *uucp requests*	**uustat**
send return mail when you're on *vacation*	**vacation**
force shell to *wait*	**wait**
count the number of *words* in text file	**wc**
return current *working directory*	**pwd**
write message to other user on the network	**write**

3

UNIX/DOS
Cross Reference

Oldtime UNIX hacks may think it heresy to include a DOS cross reference in a UNIX reference text—after all, isn't UNIX the greatest operating system ever created? We have a few good reasons to include this section, however:

- Most computer users, whether they are using UNIX or not, are somewhat familiar with DOS. In our experience, even if a computer user is using one operating system at work—say, a proprietary mainframe operating system or something like VMS—they are probably using a PC clone and DOS at home. The personal computer made personal computing affordable for the masses, and after all, DOS is one of the most popular operating systems on the face of the earth.

- Many UNIX users will be moving up from DOS. This is an unalterable fact of UNIX life. Many corporations are finding that DOS-based networks simply can't handle the large-scale computing chores handled rather effortlessly by UNIX-based networks.

- DOS has its roots in UNIX. The originators of DOS (*not* Microsoft, incidentally) patterned DOS after UNIX and used many of the same commands (such as **cd** and **echo**) while maintaining the same file

27

structure and philosophy (standard input/output plays a large role in DOS computing). Of course, this was many, many years ago, and both DOS and UNIX have changed quite a bit in response to different computing needs. For instance, DOS is heavy on disk utilities, such as **CHKDSK** and **DISKCOPY**; UNIX is heavy on networking, text-editing, and text-manipulation commands. Each system evolved to accommodate the needs of folks who ended up using it: DOS is the system of choice for single, standalone PC users, while UNIX has always dominated the multiuser corporate and academic worlds.

Don't worry if you're a DOS user and don't recognize all of the DOS commands in this list. Like UNIX, some older DOS commands have managed to hang in there despite their relative obscurity. It's safe to say that 99 percent of all DOS users have never even *heard* of the **CTTY** command, much less used it. And because this listing of DOS commands is current as of MS-DOS 6.0, many new commands (such as **MSAV**, which concerns an anti-virus utility) may be unfamiliar.

Not all DOS commands have a UNIX analog, obviously. Similarly, some UNIX commands have no parallel in the DOS world. We note cases in which there is no UNIX equivalent. And not all of the commands are *perfectly* matched; in some cases, we've listed the rough equivalent.

DOS Command	UNIX Command
APPEND	*None*
ASSIGN	*None*
ATTRIB	**chmod**
BACKUP	**cpio, tar**
BREAK	*None*
CALL	**exec**
CD	**cd**
CHCP	*None*
CHDIR	**cd**
CHKDSK	*None*
CHOICE	*None*
CLS	**clear**
COMMAND	**csh, sh**
COMP	**bdiff, cmp, diff, diff3, sdiff**
COPY	**cp**
CTTY	**stty**
DATE	**date**
DBLSPACE	*None*
DEFRAG	*None*
DEL	**rm**
DELTREE	**rm -r**
DIR	**ls**
DISKCOMP	*None*
DISKCOPY	*None*
DOSKEY	**history** (Korn and Bourne shells)
DOSSHELL	*None*
ECHO	**echo**
EDIT	**vi**
EXIT	*None*
EXPAND	**uncompress, unpack**
FASTHELP	**apropos, man, whatis**
FASTOPEN	*None*

DOS Command	UNIX Command
FC	**bdiff, cmp, diff, diff3, sdiff**
FDISK	**bdiff, cmp, diff, diff3, sdiff**
FIND	**find**
FOR	**for** (shell command)
FORMAT	*None*
GOTO	**goto** (C shell)
GRAFTABL	*None*
GRAPHICS	*None*
HELP	**apropos, man, whatis**
IF	**if** (shell command)
INTERLNK	*None*
INTERSVR	*None*
JOIN	*None*
KEYB	*None*
LABEL	*None*
LOADFIX	*None*
LOADHIGH	*None* (thankfully)
MEM	*None*
MEMMAKER	*None*
MIRROR	*None*
MKDIR	**mkdir**
MODE	**stty, tty**
MORE	**more, pg**
MOVE	**mv**
MSAV	*None*
MSBACKUP	**cpio, tar**
MSD	*None*
NLSFUNC	*None*
PATH	**setenv PATH** (C shell), **setpath** (Bourne shell)
PAUSE	**sleep**
POWER	*None*
PRINT	**pr**
PROMPT	**PS1**
RECOVER	*None*

DOS Command	UNIX Command
REM	#
RENAME	**move**
REPLACE	*None*
RESTORE	**cpio, tar**
RMDIR	**rmdir**
SET	**env**
SETVER	*None*
SHARE	*None*
SHIFT	*None*
SMARTDRV	*None*
SORT	**sort**
SUBST	*None*
SYS	*None*
TIME	**date**
TREE	*None*
TYPE	**more, page, pg**
UNDELETE	*None* (unfortunately)
UNFORMAT	*None*
VER	**uname**
VERIFY	*None*
VOL	*None*
VSAFE	*None*
XCOPY	**cp**
XTREE	**mkdir**

4

UNIX Commands A to Z

Here is an alphabetical listing of the commands covered in Chapters 5 and 6. This certainly does not comprise a list of every available UNIX command—life's too short, and we're too young, to try to compile such a list. Most UNIX users aren't going to use all the commands listed here, much less an addition set of commands whose obscurity is rivaled only by their lack of usefulness in everyday computing chores.

This list is aimed toward the majority of UNIX users who want to get on with their work and not let the operating system interfere with their chores. To that end, this list represents the UNIX commands most users are most likely to use.

Command	Section
apropos	General-Purpose Commands
at	System-Administration Commands
atq	System-Administration Commands
atrm	System-Administration Commands
awk	General-Purpose Commands
banner	Printing Commands
basename	General-Purpose Commands
batch	System-Administration Commands
bc	General-Purpose Commands
bdftopcf	Graphical Commands
bdiff	File-Manipulation Commands
bitmap	Graphical Commands
cal	General-Purpose Commands
calctool	Graphical Commands
calendar	General-Purpose Commands
cancel	Printing Commands
cat	File-Manipulation Commands
cc	General-Purpose Commands
cd	File-Manipulation Commands
chgrp	System-Administration Commands
chmod	General-Purpose Commands
chown	File-Manipulation Commands
clear	General-Purpose Commands
clock	Graphical Commands
cm	Graphical Commands
cmdtool	Graphical Commands
cmp	File-Manipulation Commands
col	Text-Processing Commands
comm	File-Manipulation Commands
compress	File-Manipulation Commands
cpio	System-Administration Commands
crontab	System-Administration Commands
crypt	File-Manipulation Commands
csh	General-Purpose Commands

Command	Section
csplit	File-Manipulation Commands
ct	Internet/Communications Commands
cu	Internet/Communications Commands
cut	Text-Processing Commands
date	General-Purpose Commands
dc	General-Purpose Commands
deroff	Text-Processing Commands
diff	File-Manipulation Commands
diff3	File-Manipulation Commands
dircmp	File-Manipulation Commands
df	General-Purpose Commands
dtcalc	Graphical Commands
dtcm	Graphical Commands
dtfile	Graphical Commands
dthelpview	Graphical Commands
dticon	Graphical Commands
dtksh	Graphical Commands
dtlp	Graphical Commands
dtmail	Graphical Commands
dtpad	Graphical Commands
dtstyle	Graphical Commands
dtterm	Graphical Commands
dtwm	Graphical Commands
du	General-Purpose Commands
echo	General-Purpose Commands
ed	Text-Processing Commands
egrep	File-Manipulation Commands
env	General-Purpose Commands
eqn	Text-Processing Commands
exit	General-Purpose Commands
fgrep	File-Manipulation Commands
file	File-Manipulation Commands
filemgr	Graphical Commands
finger	General-Purpose Commands

Command	Section
fmt	Text-Processing Commands
fold	Text-Processing Commands
fsinfo	Graphical Commands
fslsfonts	Graphical Commands
fstobdf	Graphical Commands
ftp	Internet/Communications Commands
ghostview	Graphical Commands
grep	File-Manipulation Commands
groups	General-Purpose Commands
head	File-Manipulation Commands
iconedit	Graphical Commands
id	General-Purpose Commands
join	File-Manipulation Commands
kill	General-Purpose Commands
ksh	General-Purpose Commands
listusers	General-Purpose Commands
ln	File-Manipulation Commands
login	System-Administration Commands
logname	Internet/Communications Commands
lp	Printing Commands
lpsched	Printing Commands
lpshut	Printing Commands
lpstat	Printing Commands
ls	File-Manipulation Commands
mailtool	Graphical Commands
mailx	Internet/Communications Commands
man	General-Purpose Commands
mesg	Internet/Communications Commands
mkdir	File-Manipulation Commands
mkfontdir	Graphical Commands
more	File-Manipulation Commands
mv	File-Manipulation Commands
mwm	Graphical Commands
nawk	General-Purpose Commands

Command	Section
neqn	Text-Processing Commands
newform	Text-Processing Commands
newgrp	System-Administration Commands
news	General-Purpose Commands
nice	General-Purpose Commands
nl	Text-Processing Commands
nohup	General-Purpose Commands
notify	Internet/Communications Commands
nroff	Text-Processing Commands
oclock	Graphical Commands
olwm	Graphical Commands
openwin	Graphical Commands
pack	File-Manipulation Commands
page	File-Manipulation Commands
passwd	General-Purpose Commands
paste	Text-Processing Commands
pcat	File-Manipulation Commands
pr	Printing Commands
ps	General-Purpose Commands
pwd	General-Purpose Commands
rcp	Internet/Communications Commands
rlogin	Internet/Communications Commands
rm	File-Manipulation Commands
rmdir	File-Manipulation Commands
rsh	Internet/Communications Commands
ruptime	General-Purpose Commands
rwho	General-Purpose Commands
script	General-Purpose Commands
sdiff	File-Manipulation Commands
sh	General-Purpose Commands
shelltool	Graphical Commands
shutdown	System-Administration Commands
sleep	General-Purpose Commands
sort	Text-Processing Commands

Command	Section
spell	Text-Processing Commands
split	File-Manipulation Commands
startx	Graphical Commands
strings	File-Manipulation Commands
stty	System-Administration Commands
su	General-Purpose Commands
sum	Internet/Communications Commands
tabs	Text-Processing Commands
tail	File-Manipulation Commands
talk	Internet/Communications Commands
tapetool	Graphical Commands
tar	File-Manipulation Commands
tbl	Text-Processing Commands
tee	General-Purpose Commands
telnet	Internet/Communications Commands
textedit	Graphical Commands
time	General-Purpose Commands
timex	General-Purpose Commands
toolwait	Graphical Commands
touch	File-Manipulation Commands
tput	System-Administration Commands
tr	Text-Processing Commands
troff	Text-Processing Commands
tty	System-Administration Commands
twm	Graphical Commands
umask	General-Purpose Commands
uname	General-Purpose Commands
uncompress	File-Manipulation Commands
uniq	Text-Processing Commands
unpack	File-Manipulation Commands
uucp	Internet/Communications Commands
uudecode	Internet/Communications Commands
uuencode	Internet/Communications Commands
uulog	Internet/Communications Commands

Command	Section
uuname	Internet/Communications Commands
uustat	Internet/Communications Commands
uux	Internet/Communications Commands
vacation	Internet/Communications Commands
vi	Text-Processing Commands
wait	General-Purpose Commands
wall	Internet/Communications Commands
wc	Text-Processing Commands
whatis	General-Purpose Commands
who	General-Purpose Commands
write	Internet/Communications Commands
X	Graphical Commands
xauth	Graphical Commands
xbiff	Graphical Commands
xcalc	Graphical Commands
xclipboard	Graphical Commands
xclock	Graphical Commands
xcmap	Graphical Commands
xconsole	Graphical Commands
xditview	Graphical Commands
xdm	Graphical Commands
xdpr	Graphical Commands
xdpyinfo	Graphical Commands
xdvi	Graphical Commands
xedit	Graphical Commands
xfd	Graphical Commands
xfontsel	Graphical Commands
xfs	Graphical Commands
xhost	Graphical Commands
xinit	Graphical Commands
xkill	Graphical Commands
xload	Graphical Commands
xlock	Graphical Commands
xlogo	Graphical Commands

Command	Section
xlsfonts	Graphical Commands
xmag	Graphical Commands
xman	Graphical Commands
xpr	Graphical Commands
xprop	Graphical Commands
xrdb	Graphical Commands
xv	Graphical Commands
xwd	Graphical Commands
xwininfo	Graphical Commands
xwud	Graphical Commands

5

UNIX Commands, Organized by Group

This chapter organizes UNIX commands by group and function. We think you'll find this method of organization best suited for your daily tasks; most people run across a problem and then try to solve it. This method of organization allows you to hone in on the general topic; from there you can browse through the appropriate commands to find the one that best serves your needs.

The seven categories are:

- General-Purpose Commands
- File-Manipulation Commands
- Text-Processing Commands
- Printing Commands
- Communication Commands
- Graphics Commands
- Programming Commands

Each command's explanation follows the same structure. An initial line shows how you would use this command as part of a command line. For instance, some commands require you to list a filename, while others support various options. In the instances where you need to enter information specific to your circumstances—such as filenames and options—these variables are printed in *italics*.

Additional information includes the command's purpose (a short chunk of text in which the commands appear in **boldface**), an example (where appropriate; these are command lines that would be directly entered in your system), and related commands (where appropriate).

These commands have been tested with a wide range of UNIX systems (for a complete list, see the Introduction). We've tried to flag instances where a command may not be available on all systems. In addition, a few commands work differently depending on whether you're using BSD UNIX (referred to as BSD in this chapter) or System V UNIX (referred to as SV), while other commands were newly introduced in System V Release 4 (referred to as SVR4).

General-Purpose Commands

These general-purpose commands are geared to the every-day tasks of UNIX usage and cover a wide variety of tasks.

apropos *keyword(s)*

PURPOSE

Returns information about the specified *keyword(s)* from the online manual pages. Not available on all systems.

EXAMPLE

```
$ apropos shell
```

OPTIONS

None.

RELATED COMMANDS

man	Returns information from online-manual pages.
whatis	Returns information from online-manual pages.
xman	Returns information from online-manual pages.

basename *pathname suffix*

PURPOSE

Returns only the actual filename when presented with a pathname. If a suffix is specified, the suffix will also be removed. Generally, **basename** is used in shell scripts and in other situations calling for command substitution.

EXAMPLE

```
$ basename /usr/users/kevin/files/1997/stuff
stuff
```

OPTIONS

None.

bc *options files*

PURPOSE

This calculator command supports a wide range of commands and conditions. **bc** is also a language very similar to the C programming language.

After running the **bc** command, the command prompt disappears, and keywords, symbols, and operations can be entered directly.

bc is an involved tool that's far too complicated for this introductory work. There's a whole set of specialized commands that are not even listed here, as you'll see from the short example. See the Bibliography for a list of UNIX tutorials that should cover **bc** in some form.

EXAMPLE

```
$ bc
scale=5
sqrt((66*6)/55)
2.6832
quit
```

OPTIONS

-c   Compiles the specified *filename*.

-l   Makes the math library available. (Note: When you invoke this option, you automatically set the scale to 20.)

COMMON INSTRUCTIONS

+	Addition.
-	Subtraction.
/	Division.
*	Multiplication.
%	Remainder.
^	Exponentiation.
sqrt(n**)**	Square root.
scale=n	Sets scale (after decimal point).
ibase=n	Sets input base (default is 10).
obase=x	Sets output base (default is 10).
define a(b)	Defines the function a with the argument b.
for, if, while	Statement keywords.

OTHER OPERATORS AND SYMBOLS

assignment	=+ =- =* =/ =^ =
relational	< <= > >= == !=
unary	- ++ —

OTHER SYMBOLS

/* */	Comment lines.
{}	Brackets statements.
[]	Array index.
text	Prints text.

General
Purpose

Continued

MATH-LIBRARY FUNCTIONS

s	sine
c	cosine
a	arctangent
e	exponential; base e
l	natural logarithm
j(n,x**)**	Bessel function

RELATED COMMAND

dc	Desk calculator.

cal *option*

PURPOSE

Displays the current month in calendar form. If a year is specified, a 12-month calendar is printed. If a month and year are specified, that specific month is printed.

 Don't confuse the cal command with the calendar command.

 The command cal 94 displays the calendar for the year A.D. 94, not 1994. Also, the calendar is based on British/American convention. Try cal 1752 to see the jump to the Gregorian calendar.

EXAMPLES

```
cal
cal 11 1994
cal 1997
cal 1752
```

OPTIONS

month   Specific month, in numerical form.
year   Specific year.

RELATED COMMANDS

calendar   Sets up a personal calendar.
date   Displays current date and time.

General Purpose

calendar *option*

PURPOSE

This rudimentary personal organizer allows you to store events in a file named **calendar**. On the current day, the **calendar** command will scan the **calendar** file for all events occurring on that day. (Many users place the **calendar** commands in their startup files.)

The events must be listed on one line, with the date in one of three formats:

```
11/12
Nov. 12
November 12
```

EXAMPLES

```
11/12   drinks with Eric
11/15   drinks with Eric
11/18   drinks with Eric
```

If this were your **calendar** file, you'd be reminded of these important engagements when you ran the **calendar** command on November 12, November 15, and November 18.

Continued

OPTION

- Privileged users can use this option to scan the system for files named **calendar** in login directories, automatically sending corresponding events from each file to the appropriate user.

RELATED COMMANDS

cal	Returns a monthly or yearly calendar.
cm	Manage appointments
date	Displays current date and time.
dtcm	Manage appointments

chmod *option mode filename(s)*

PURPOSE

Changes the file-access permissions on a given file or files, or on the contents of an entire subdirectory. Only the owner of the file or a privileged user can change the mode of a file.

There are two ways to change permissions: through symbolic or numeric form. The numeric form is used to set absolute permission values, while the symbolic form is used to set values relative to the current value.

To get the current permissions, use the **ls** command, which is covered elsewhere in this chapter.

EXAMPLE USING NUMERIC FORM

```
$ chmod 744 kevin.report
```

This example uses the **chmod** command on the file **kevin.report** to set a permission status where the owner can read, write, and execute a file, while the file's specified group and all other users can read the file but cannot execute the file or write to it.

The value of *744* comes from adding together the mode values found in the next section, "Modes." The lowest possible value is 000—which means no one can read, write, or execute the file—while the highest possible value is 777, where everyone can read, write, and execute the file. Here's the exact arithmetic used to arrive at 744:

Continued

400	Owner has read permission.
200	Owner has write permission.
100	Owner has execute permission.
040	Group has read permission.
004	World has read permission.
———	
744	

The next time you run an **ls** command (using the long form, of course) on the file **kevin.report**, the permissions would be set as:

```
rwxr--r--
```

See Chapter 1, "UNIX Overview: Commands and Structures," for a more in-depth explanation of file-access permissions.

MODES

The *mode* is an octal number in the following format:

NUMBER	MEANING
400	Owner has read permission.
200	Owner has write permission.
100	Owner has execute permission.
040	Group has read permission.
020	Group has write permission.

General Purpose

Continued

010	Group has execute permission.
004	World has read permission.
002	World has write permission.
001	World has execute permission.

Add together the numbers for the permissions you want. For example, 423 means that you, the user, can read the file, users in your group can write the file, and the rest of the world can write and execute the file. (Note that you usually need read permission to execute a file.)

THE SYMBOLIC FORM

When permissions are set in this manner, the modes are entered in symbolic form, but the structure of the command remains the same. Instead of using numerals in the mode field, you'd use one of the following symbols:

SYMBOL	MEANING
u	User (who actually owns the file).
g	Group.
o	Other.
all	All (this is the default).
+	Add a permission to the current permissions.
-	Remove a permission from the current permissions.
=	Assign an absolute permission irrespective of the current permission.
r	Read.
w	Write.
x	Execute.
l	Mandatory lock during access.

Continued

You can set more than one mode at a time, making sure that the settings are separated by a comma (with no spaces on either side of it). In addition, you can set permissions for more than one set of users in the same mode statement, as shown in the following examples.

EXAMPLES USING SYMBOLIC FORM

```
$ chmod u+x kevin.report
```

(This allows the owner of the file **kevin.report** to execute the file.)

```
$ chmod u-x kevin.report
```

(This removes the ability of the owner of the file **kevin.report** to execute the file.)

```
$ chmod u+x,go-w file.report
```

(This allows the owner of the file **kevin.report** to execute the file, while removing the permissions of the group and all other users to write to the file.)

OPTION

-R   Recursively changes through subdirectories and files.

RELATED COMMANDS

chgrp   Changes group membership.
chown   Changes file ownership.
newgrp   Changes to a new working group.

General
Purpose

clear

PURPOSE

Clears the screen.

EXAMPLE

```
$ clear
```

csh

PURPOSE

Starts the C shell, one of many UNIX command-line interfaces. See Chapter 7, "Shell Commands and Variables," for more information.

date *option +format*

date *option string* (for privileged users)

PURPOSE

Displays current date in a wide variety of formats (as the list of options indicates). Or, for those with privileged status, the **date** command can be used to set the system date and time.

EXAMPLES

```
$ date
```

(This returns the current date and time.)

```
$ date -u
```

(This returns the date and time in universal time, or Greenwich Mean Time.)

```
$ date +%A
```

(This returns the date and time with the day of the week spelled out.)

```
$ date 1115063094
```

(This sets the date and time to November 15, 6:30 a.m., 1994. Only privileged users can change the system date and time.)

Continued

OPTION

-u   Returns the date and time in universal time, or Greenwich Mean Time (GMT).

OPTIONS (PRIVILEGED USERS)

-a[-]s,f   Adjusts the time by seconds (s) or fractions of seconds (f). The default is to adjust the time forward; use - to adjust the time backward.

[MMdd]hhmm[yy]]   Changes the date and time (using month, day, hour, minute, and year).

FORMATS

%a	Day of the week abbreviated (Sun, Mon, et al.).
%A	Day of the week spelled out (Sunday, Monday, et al.).
%b	Month abbreviated (Jan, Feb, et al.). (Same as **%h**.)
%B	Month spelled out (January, February, et al.).
%c	Date and time for a particular country.
%d	Day of the month in two digits (01–31).
%D	Date returned in *mm/dd/yy* format.
%e	Day of the month as numeral (1–31).
%h	Month abbreviated (Jan, Feb, et al.). (Same as **%b**.)
%H	Hours returned in military time (00–24).
%I	Hours returned in nonmilitary time (0–12).
%j	Day returned in Julian date (001–365).
%m	Month returned as a number (01 for January, 02 for February, et al.).
%M	Minutes (0–59).
%n	Insert a newline.

General
Purpose

Continued

%p	Time of day indicated (AM or PM).
%S	Seconds (0–59).
%t	Inserts a tab.
%T	Time in *hh:mm:ss* format.
%U	Week returned as a number (0–51), with week starting on Sunday.
%w	Day of the week as a number (0 for Sunday, 1 for Monday, et al.).
%W	Week returned as a number (0–51), with week starting on a Monday.
%x	Country-specific time format.
%X	Country-specific date format.
%y	Year returned in two digits (94).
%Y	Year returned in four digits (1994).
%Z	Time zone.

dc *file*

PURPOSE

Desk calculator performs arbitrary-precision integer arithmetic, either from commands contained in a file or from keyboard input. Normally this command is not used on its own. The **bc** command acts as a friendly front end to the **dc** command, while the **dc** command works as a Reverse Polish calculator—commands and operators follow the numbers they affect. Most people are not used to working in this format and prefer working with the more straightforward **bc** calculator.

EXAMPLES

```
$ 7 10 * p
70
```

(This multiplies 7 by 10 and then prints the result.)

```
$ 27-p
```

(This subtracts 27 from the previous number.)

COMMANDS

+	Adds last number to previous number.
-	Subtracts last number from previous number.
*	Multiplies last number from previous number.
/	Divides last number from previous number.
c	Clears all values.
i	Changes input base.

Continued

k	Sets scale factor (number of digits after decimal).
o	Changes output base.
p	Prints current result.
q	Quits **dc**.
v	Finds square root.

RELATED COMMAND

bc   Calculator.

df *options system_name*

PURPOSE

Displays information about the amount of free disk space on a file system or a file system specified by *system_name*. A series of options allows you to display the total amount of free space (in kilobytes or disk blocks) or the total disk space.

EXAMPLES

```
$ df
```

(This returns the amount of free disk space in each directory.)

```
$ df -t
```

(This returns the amount of allocated space, as well as the free disk space.)

OPTIONS

-b	Displays the amount of free disk space in kilobytes.
-e	Displays the number of free files. Not available on all systems.
-F *type*	Used to return information about unmounted file systems, specified by *type*. (A list of available types can be found in **/etc/vfstab** on some versions of UNIX.)
-g	Returns the entire **statvfs** structure for all unmounted file systems. (This command is new in SVR4.)
-k	Prints the amount of allocation in kilobytes.

General Purpose

Continued

-l	Prints information only about local file systems.
-n	Displays the *type* of file system. Not available on all systems.
-t	Displays free space as well as allocated space. Not available on all systems.

RELATED COMMAND

du	Displays disk-space usage.

du *options files directories*

PURPOSE

Displays the amount of disk space used by a directory (and all its subdirectories) in blocks (usually 512 bytes each). The default is the current directory.

OPTIONS

-a	Displays information about all files, not only directories.
-r	Reports on files and directories **du** cannot open.
-s	Silent mode. Displays only totals.

RELATED COMMAND

df	Displays disk free-space information.

General
Purpose

echo *option string*

PURPOSE

Echoes text or values to standard output. Technically, **echo** exists in three forms: as a UNIX command (contained in **/bin/echo**), as a C shell command, and as a Bourne shell command. There are a few small differences: the C shell version does not support the **-n** option, nor does it support escape characters. However, the three are usually used interchangeably, and that is the approach used here.

EXAMPLES

```
$ echo "Good morning!"
```

(This would print the string *Good Morning* to the screen.)

```
$ echo "This is a test" | lp
```

(This would print the line *This is a test* to the line printer.)

OPTION

-n   Do not end the output with a newline. (This does not apply to the C shell version.)

CONTROL CHARACTERS

\b   Backspace.

\c   No newline.

\f   Form feed.

Continued

\n	Newline.
\r	Carriage return.
\t	Tab.
\v	Vertical tab.
\\	Backslash.
\n	ASCII code of any character.

General
Purpose

env *option [variable=value] command*

PURPOSE

Displays the current user environment variables with their values or makes changes to environment variables. The term *environment* refers to a variety of variable settings used by the command shell, including the login directory, default shell, login name, terminal type, and command path. When you change these settings, you are said to be changing the *environment*.

This command works differently in the C shell. See Chapter 7, "Shell Commands and Variables," for more information.

EXAMPLES

```
$ env SHELL=/bin/csh
```

(This sets your default shell to the C shell.)

```
$ env HOME=/usr/users/kevin/notes
```

(This sets your home directory to **/usr/users/kevin/notes**.)

OPTION

-              Ignores the current environment variable.

exit

PURPOSE

Quits the current session. This is actually a shell command, with different options based on the shell version. See Chapter 7, "Shell Commands and Variables," for more information on shell-specific implementations.

finger *options user(s)*

PURPOSE

Returns the following information about users with accounts on the system: username, full name, terminal, terminal access, time of login, and phone number. In addition, **finger** grabs information from the user's login shell, **.plan** file, and **.project** file. Information is returned in long display or short display.

The **finger** command searches for information based on a specific username or general first and last names. For instance, a search of the name *smith* on a large system will probably yield quite a few responses. The use of the **finger** command with no username will return a list of all users currently logged on the system.

EXAMPLE

```
$ finger erc
Login name: erc        In real life: Eric F. Johnson
(612) 555-5555
Directory:/home/erc              Shell:/usr/bin/ksh
Last login Wed Nov 10 12:14:45 on term/07
Project: X Window Programming
erc       term/07     Nov 11 19:45
```

Continued

OPTIONS

-b	Long display, without information about home directory and shell.
-f	Short display, sans header.
-h	Long display, without information gleaned from the **.project** file.
-i	Shows "idle" status: username, terminal, time of login, and idle lines.
-l	Long display.
-m	Matches the username exactly, with no searching of first or last names.
-p	Long display, without information gleaned from the **.plan** file.
-q	Quick display of username, terminal, and time of login (with no searching of first or last names).
-s	Short format.
-w	Short format, without the user's first name.

RELATED COMMAND

who	Displays or changes usernames.

groups *user*

PURPOSE

Returns a list of the groups a *user* belongs to (the default is a listing of your groups).

RELATED COMMANDS

chgrp   Changes group.
newgrp   Changes group.

id *option*

PURPOSE

Displays your user ID and username, as well as your group ID and groupname.

OPTION

-a   Displays all groups.

RELATED COMMANDS

logname   Displays logname.
who   Displays users.

kill *options PID*

PURPOSE

Kills a current process (specified by a PID and returned by the **ps** command), as long as you own the process or are a privileged user. This command is also built into the Korn, Bourne, and C shells, although there are slight differences.

kill -9 is the most serious form of all.

OPTIONS

-l   Lists the signal names.

-signal   The *signal* can be a number (returned by **ps -f**) or a name (returned by **kill -l**).

RELATED COMMAND

ps   Process status.

ksh

PURPOSE

Starts the Korn shell, one of UNIX's many command-line interfaces. See Chapter 7, "Shell Commands and Variables," for more information.

listusers *options*

PURPOSE

Returns a listing of usernames and IDs. Not available on all systems.

OPTIONS

-g *groupname*	Returns members of *groupname*.
-l *login*	Returns list of users with the name *login*.

man *command*

PURPOSE

Displays the online-manual page for a command. There's actually a lot more to this command, but most of it involves either Solaris 2.0 or advanced options geared toward more experienced users. If you want more information about the **man** command specific to your system, use the **man man** command.

RELATED COMMANDS

apropos   Returns information for a specific keyword.
whatis   Returns information from online-manual pages.

news *options newsitem(s)*

PURPOSE

Displays all news items distributed systemwide. These items are usually stored in **/usr/news** or **/var/news** and set up by the system administrator.

OPTIONS

-a	Displays all of the news items.
-n	Displays the names of all of the news items.
-s	Displays a count of all of the news items.

nice *option command arguments*

PURPOSE

Runs a command nicely by giving it a very low priority.
This is used for involved commands that can be run over a
period of some time (such as over lunch) without causing
you any inconvenience.

OPTION

-*n*   Specifies *n* as the decrement in priority.
                     The default is 10.

nohup *command arguments &*

PURPOSE

Keeps a command running even if you log off the system.

passwd *options*
passwd *options user* (privileged users)

PURPOSE

Sets the user's password.

OPTIONS

-s Displays current password information:

user	Username.
status	Password status: **NP** (no password), **PS** (password), or **LK** (locked).
mm/dd/yy	Date when last changed.
min	Minimum number of days before password must be changed.
max	Maximum number of days before password must be changed.
notice	Number of days before you are given notice that your password must be changed.

OPTIONS (PRIVILEGED USERS)

-a	Displays password information for all users.
-d	Stop prompting user for password.
-f	Force user to change password.
-l	Lock user password.
-n	Sets number of days that must pass before user can rechange password.
-w	Sets number of days before user is warned that the password expires.
-x	Sets number of days before password expires.

RELATED COMMAND

login Login system.

General
Purpose

ps *options*

PURPOSE

Returns the status of all current processes. When used by itself, **ps** returns basic information about a process by **PID** (process ID), **TTY**, **TIME**, and **COMMAND**. A rather long list of options allows you to more effectively find any additional information you might need.

In BSD UNIX, the options are different; for instance, use **ps -aux** instead of **ps -ef**.

OPTIONS

-a	Displays all processes, except group leaders and those not controlled by a terminal.
-c	Displays information about scheduler priorities.
-d	Displays all processes, except group leaders.
-e	Displays information on every process.
-f	Displays full information about processes, including **UID**, **PID**, **PPID**, **C**, **STIME**, **TTY**, **TIME**, and **COMMAND**.
-g *list*	Displays processes for *list* of group leader IDs.
-j	Displays session and process group IDs.
-l	Displays a long listing, which includes such information as priorities set with the **nice** command—and much, much more.
-p *list*	Displays processes whose process IDs are contained in *list*.
-s *list*	Displays processes whose session leaders are contained in *list*.
-t *list*	Displays processes whose terminals are contained in *list*.
-u *list*	Displays processes whose users are contained in *list*.

RELATED COMMANDS

kill	Kills a process.
nice	Runs command at lower priority.

pwd

PURPOSE

Returns the current working directory.

OPTIONS

None.

RELATED COMMAND

cd   Changes directory.

General
Purpose

ruptime *options*

PURPOSE

Shows the status of all machines connected to the network. The resulting table shows the name of each host, whether the host is up or down, the amount of time it has been up or down, the number of users on the host, and the average load for that machine.

OPTIONS

-a	Includes all users, even those whose machines have been idle for more than an hour.
-l	Sorts by load.
-r	Reverses sort order.
-t	Sorts by uptime.
-u	Sorts by number of users.

rwho *option*

PURPOSE

Shows who is logged on all machines on the network.

OPTION

-a   Includes all users, even those whose machines have
                      been idle for more than an hour.

RELATED COMMAND

who   Shows users logged on the network.

script *option filename*

PURPOSE

Saves a copy of your current computing session. (Actually, this starts a new session and logs it.) The default storage file is *typescript*, although you can change that on the command line.

Script saves all characters that appear on your screen, including control and escape characters. The recording ends when you type **exit** or **Ctrl-D** to end the session.

OPTION

-a   Appends output to the new *filename*.

sh

PURPOSE

Starts the Bourne shell. See Chapter 7, "Shell Commands and Variables," for more information.

sleep   Suspends Session

sleep *seconds*

PURPOSE

Suspends the system for a specified number of seconds
before running another command. This is handy when
working with shell scripts.

RELATED COMMAND

wait   Waits for the completion of a process.

su *option user shell_args*

PURPOSE

Allows you to become another user without logging on and off the system, suspending your current shell while logging you in as the substitute user. The most common use of **su** is to temporarily become the superuser to perform privileged administrative commands.

EXAMPLE

If you wanted to log in as **kevin** (which is an experience every person should have in their lifetime) while already logged in the system as **erc**, you'd enter the following:

```
$ su kevin
```

The system would then prompt you for the password for user *kevin*.

OPTION

-                Fully become the substitute user by adopting the
                 environment.

RELATED COMMAND

login   Login system.

tee *options file(s)*

PURPOSE

Sends standard output to a specified file in addition to displaying the output on the screen. Without the use of **tee**, there's no way to redirect output from a command *both* to the screen and to a file, or to two separate commands. This command is never used on its own, but rather as part of a longer command line.

EXAMPLE

```
$ spell textfile | tee badwords
```

(This runs the **spell** command on the file **textfile**, sending the output to a file named **badwords**.)

```
$ ls | tee textfile | wc
```

(This runs the **ls** command to generate a directory listing, sending the output to **tee**, which writes the listing to the file **textfile** and also sends the listing to the **wc** command, which displays a count of the lines, words, and bytes in the listing.)

OPTIONS

-a	Appends output to *file(s)*.
-i	Ignores system interrupts.

time *command*

PURPOSE

Runs a specified command and reports back on the time it took to run the command (elapsed time, user time, system time) in seconds. An expanded version, **timex**, is available on most UNIX systems.

EXAMPLE

```
$ time ls
```

(This runs the **ls** command, which generates a directory listing; **time** then prints the time it took to run **ls**.)

OPTIONS

None.

RELATED COMMAND

timex   Displays time for running a command.

timex *options command*

PURPOSE

Runs a specified command and reports back on the time it took to run the command (elapsed time, user time, system time) in seconds, with options for returning the number of blocks read and written, system activity, and other accounting information. This is an expanded version of the **time** command.

OPTIONS

-o	Shows number of blocks used and characters transferred.
-p *suboptions*	Returns process activity for *command* through one or more of the suboptions:
-f	Shows fork/exit flag and exit status.
-h	Shows "hog" factor: CPU time divided by elapsed time.
-k	Shows kcore time in minutes.
-m	Shows mean core size (default).
-r	Shows CPU use comparisons.
-t	Shows CPU and system times.
-s	Returns total system activity while *command* is run.

RELATED COMMAND

time	Displays time for running a command.

umask *values*

PURPOSE

Creates or returns the current value of the file-creation mask, which determines default values for new files. This value, also known as *permissions*, determines who has access to files and directories on the system. **umask** sets the default permissions for new files; you change the permissions for an existing file with **chmod**. On its own, **umask** returns the current default value.

This command is the functional opposite of **chmod**. When *ugo* is used with **umask**, permissions are denied for everyone; when *ugo* is used with **chmod**, permissions are granted.

However, **umask** uses a different method of specifying permissions—by numbers rather than symbols:

UMASK NUMBER	FILE PERMISSION	DIRECTORY PERMISSION
0	rw-	rwx
1	rw-	rw-
2	r--	r-x
3	r--	r--
4	-w-	-wx
5	-w-	-w-
6	---	--x
7	---	---

General
Purpose

Continued

EXAMPLES

```
$ umask 137
```

(This results in a file permission of -rw-r-----.)

RELATED COMMAND

chmod   Changes permissions.

uname *options*

PURPOSE

Returns the UNIX system name. On BSD systems, you'll have the **hostname** command instead.

 Do not confuse the uname command with the uuname command.

EXAMPLE

```
$ uname -a
Sun OS eric 5.3 Generic sun4M sparc
```

OPTIONS

-a	Reports all information (the sum of all other options).
-m	Returns the hardware name.
-n	Returns the node name.
-p	Returns the processor type.
-r	Returns the operating-system release.
-s	Returns the system name.
-v	Returns the operating-system version.

General
Purpose

wait   Wait for Job to Complete

wait *ID*

PURPOSE

Forces your shell to wait until background processes are completed before starting a new process.

OPTIONS

ID   Job-process ID.

RELATED COMMANDS

ps   Lists job processes.
sleep   Suspends execution.

whatis *command*

PURPOSE

Looks up the online-manual page for *command* and presents a one-line summary.

RELATED COMMANDS

apropos	Returns help information about command.
man	Online-manual pages.

who *options file*

PURPOSE

Displays the names and other information about users logged on the system.

OPTIONS

am I	Displays who you are (your system name).
-a	Uses all options listed here.
-b	Returns the last time and date the system was booted.
-d	Returns expired processes.
-H	Inserts column headings.
-l	Returns lines available for login.
-n*n*	Displays *n* users per line.
-p	Returns processes started by **init** that are still active.
-q	Quick who; displays only usernames.
-r	Returns run level.
-s	Returns name, line, and time fields (default).
-t	Returns the last time the system clock was updated with **clock**.
-T	Returns the state of each terminal:

	+	Any user can write to the terminal.
	-	Only system administrator can write to the terminal.
	?	Error with the terminal.

-u	Returns terminal usage in idle time.

Continued

RELATED COMMANDS

date	Displays date and time.
login	Login system.
mesg	Sets terminal access.
rwho	Remote who.

General
Purpose

File-Manipulation Commands

These commands help you in working with UNIX directories and files.

bdiff   List Differences in Files

bdiff *file1 file2 options*

PURPOSE

Compares two files and reports on the differing lines. This command actually invokes the **diff** command after dividing a file into manageable chunks; it works best with text files.

EXAMPLE

```
$ bdiff kevin.memo kevin.memo.alt
1c1
< Dear Mr. Reichard:
- - -
> Dear Scumbag:
```

OPTIONS

-n   Divides the files into segments *n* lines long. This affects the values returned regarding specific differing lines, as the example shows.

-s   Suppresses error messages.

RELATED COMMANDS

cmp   Compares two files and tells you if the files are different.

diff   Compares files and reports *all* differing lines.

diff3   Compares three files.

sdiff   Compares files side by side.

cat *options file(s)*

PURPOSE

This very handy command performs several frequently used chores:

- Combines several files into a new file (using the > operator).

- Appends other files to an existing file (using the >> operator).

- Displays a file when no operators are specified.

- Copies a file to a new name (using the > operator).

- Creates a new text file without the fuss of a text editor.

EXAMPLES

```
$ cat kevin.report
```

(The contents of the file **kevin.report** would be displayed nonstop on the screen.)

```
$ cat kevin.report kevin.memo
```

(The contents of the files **kevin.report** and **kevin.memo** would be displayed nonstop on the screen.)

```
$ cat kevin.report kevin.memo > kevin.words
```

File Manipulation
Commands

Continued

The contents of the files **kevin.report** and **kevin.memo** would be combined into a new file named **kevin.words**, in the order in which they appear on the command line.)

```
$ cat kevin.report.old > kevin.report.new
```

(The contents of **kevin.report.old** are copied into the new file named **kevin.report.new**.)

```
$ cat > kevin.report.1994
```

(**Cat** creates a new file named **kevin.report.1994** and places all keyboard input into that file, halting input when the user types **Ctrl-D**.)

```
$ cat kevin.report >> kevin.memo
```

(The contents of **kevin.report** are appended to the end of the file **kevin.memo**.)

```
$ cat - >> kevin.report
```

(Keyboard input is appended to the end of the file **kevin.report**.)

If you're not careful about how you use **cat**, you could overwrite the contents of one file with keyboard entry or the contents of another file. For instance, the command

```
$ cat - > kevin.report
```

replaces the current contents of **kevin.report** with keyboard input.

Continued

OPTIONS

-	Used as a substitute for a filename, - allows for keyboard entry to be appended to an existing file. Press **Ctrl-D** to end the keyboard entry.
-s (SV)	Silent mode; suppresses information about nonexistent files.
-s (BSD)	Removes blank lines from the file.
-u	Output is unbuffered; default is buffered, which means that characters are displayed in blocks.
-v	Prints nonprinting characters, such as control characters, except for tabs, form feeds, and newlines.
-ve	Prints nonprinting characters, such as control characters, except for tabs and form feeds, while newlines appear as dollar signs ($).
-vt	Prints nonprinting characters, such as control characters, except for newlines, while tabs appear as ^I and form feeds as ^L.
-vet	Prints all nonprinting characters.

RELATED COMMANDS

cp	Copies files.
more	Displays files one screen at a time.
page	Displays files one page at a time.
pg	Displays files one page at a time.

File Manipulation
Commands

Continued

cd *directory*

PURPOSE

Changes current directory to a new directory. This is actually a shell command, but is usually treated as a regular UNIX command.

EXAMPLES

```
$ cd
```

(This returns you to your home directory.)

```
$ cd stuff
```

(This changes you to the subdirectory **stuff** and makes it the current directory.)

```
$ cd /usr/users/eric/private
```

(This changes your current directory to another directory named **/usr/users/eric/private**.)

```
$ cd ~/stuff/1997
```

(This moves you to a subdirectory within your home directory.)

```
$ cd ..
```

Continued

(This moves your current directory one level up in the directory hierarchy.)

OPTIONS

None.

RELATED COMMAND

pwd   Prints the name of the current directory.

 The cd command is also covered in Chapter 7, "Shell Commands and Variables."

chown *options newowner file(s)*

PURPOSE

Changes the ownership of a given file or files to a new owner. The new owner is either a user ID number or a login name (these can be found in **/etc/passwd**).

The BSD version of this command also allows the group to be changed.

EXAMPLE

```
$ chown kevin kevin.report
```

(This changes the ownership of the file **kevin.report** to kevin.)

OPTIONS

-h   Changes the ownership of a symbolic link. Not available on all systems.

-R   Recursively changes through a subdirectory and symbolic links.

RELATED COMMANDS

chmod   Changes file-access permissions.

chgrp   Changes group membership.

newgrp   Changes to a new working group.

cmp *options file1 file2*

PURPOSE

Compares the contents of two files. If the files are different, **cmp** will return the byte position and line number of the first difference between the two files. If there is no difference in the files, **cmp** returns nothing.

The **cmp** command works on all files, not just text files. Similar commands, such as **diff** and **comm**, work only with text files.

EXAMPLE

```
$ cmp kevin,report kevin.memo
kevin.report kevin.memo differ: char 31, line 2
```

OPTIONS

-l	Displays the byte position and the differing characters for *all* differences within the file.
-s	Works silently, returning only the exit codes and not the instances of differences. The exit code is one of the following:
0	Files are identical
1	Files are different
2	One of the files is unreadable

RELATED COMMANDS

comm	Compares files line by line.
diff	Compares files and returns differences.
sdiff	Compares files side by side.

File Manipulation
Commands

comm *options file1 file2*

PURPOSE

Compares the contents of two presorted text files. The output is generated in three columns:

Lines found	Lines found	Lines found
in *file1*	in *file2*	in both files

EXAMPLE

```
$ comm kevin.report kevin.memo
                                    Dear Mr. Jones:
I am happy to      I am sad to
                                    report that your
                                    daughter, Felicia,
was accepted       was rejected
                                    from our fine college.
```

OPTIONS

-1	Suppresses the printing of column 1.
-2	Suppresses the printing of column 2.
-3	Suppresses the printing of column 3.
-12	Prints only column 3.
-13	Prints only column 2.
-23	Prints only column 1.

RELATED COMMANDS

cmp	Compares files byte by byte.
diff	Compares files and returns differences.
sdiff	Compares files side by side.
sort	Sorts files.

compress *options filename(s)*

PURPOSE

Compresses a file (or files), creating *filename*.Z.

OPTIONS

-b*n*	Changes the number of bits used in the compression process. The default is 16, and *n* can be set to a numeral between 9 and 16. The lower the setting, the larger the resulting compressed file.
-f	Compresses with no feedback.
-v	Returns information on how much the file was compressed.

RELATED COMMANDS

uncompress	Uncompresses a compressed file.
pack	Compresses a file or files.
unpack	Uncompresses a compressed file.
zcat	Uncompresses a compressed file.

File Manipulation
Commands

cp *options sourcefile destinationfile*

cp *options file1 directory*

cp *options directory1 directory2*

PURPOSE

Copies the contents of one file into another file with a new name, or into another directory, retaining the existing filename. It also copies the contents of one directory into a new directory.

EXAMPLE

```
$ cp kevin.memo kevin.memo.old
```

(This copies the file **kevin.memo** into a new file called **kevin.memo.old**.)

```
$ cp kevin.memo /usr/users/kevin/old_junk
```

(This copies the file **kevin.memo** into the directory **/usr/users/kevin/old_junk**.)

```
$ cp -r /usr/users/kevin/old_junk
    /usr/users/kevin/backup
```

(This copies the contents of the directory **/usr/users/kevin/old_junk** into the new directory **/usr/users/kevin/backup**.)

Continued

OPTIONS

-i	Makes sure you don't overwrite existing file.
-p	Retains existing permissions. Not available on all systems.
-r	Copies entire directory.

RELATED COMMANDS

chgrp	Changes group membership.
chmod	Changes file-access permissions.
chown	Changes file ownership.
ln	Links files.
mv	Moves or renames a file.
rm	Removes a file.

File Manipulation Commands

crypt *password option* < *file* > *encryptedfile*

PURPOSE

Takes a text file and stores it in a new encrypted file. The command also allows you to read from an encrypted file, although UNIX text editors have the ability to read encrypted files. A file is encrypted in order to avoid unauthorized access.

You need the password both to encrypt a file and to read an encrypted file, although the **-k** option allows you to set the password as an environmental variable, CRYPTKEY. The use of the **-k** option is highly frowned upon, since it lessens the security measures afforded by the **crypt** command.

The crypt command is not supported in versions of UNIX destined for export, due to U.S. security laws.

NOTE

EXAMPLE

```
$ crypt < kevin.report > kevin.new.report
```

OPTIONS

-k   Uses the password set as an environmental variable, CRYPTKEY.

csplit *options arguments*

PURPOSE

Splits a long file into a series of smaller files. When you set up the command line using **csplit**, you specify whether you want to divide up the file by size or by content—that is, through having **csplit** search for a specific expression.

The resulting files will begin with **xx**. For instance, the first file will be named **xx00**, the second named **xx01**, and so on. (However, you're limited to 100 files, so the last file in this sequence would be named **xx99**.)

EXAMPLE

```
$ csplit -k gone_wind '/^Chapter/' {30}
```

(This splits the file **gone_wind** into 30 files, all beginning with the expression "Chapter.")

OPTIONS

-f*file*	Uses *file* instead of **xx** for the beginning of filenames. (For instance, with this option enabled as **-f***this*, the first filename would be **this00**.)
-k	Keeps files even though they may not meet command-line criteria.
-s	Suppresses character counts.

Continued

ARGUMENTS

/expr/	Creates a file that begins with the current line through the line containing *expr*. You can add a suffix that ends the file a line before *expr* by appending *-1* or that ends the file a line after *expr* by appending *+1*.
%expr%	Same as */expr/*, except that no file is created for the text prior to *expr*.
line	Creates a file that begins at the current line and ends one line before line number *line*. (Note: Some documentation refers to this option as *num*. They are the same thing.)
{n}	Repeats the previous argument *n* times. Unless you specify *n*, the command line only works once.

RELATED COMMAND

split	Splits a file.

diff *options diroptions file1 file2*

PURPOSE

Compares two files and reports differing lines. The results are clear: the line numbers of the differing lines are noted, while the offending line from *file1* is marked with < and the offending line from *file2* is marked with >. Three hyphens (---) separate the contents of the two files. This command works best with text files.

 Diff cannot process large files; use bdiff in those situations.

EXAMPLE

```
$ diff erc.memo erc.memo.1112
1c1
< Dear Boss:
- - -
> Dear Mr. King:
4c4
< This idea should be nuked.
- - -
> —Eric
```

OPTIONS

-b	Ignores blanks at the end of line.
-c	Produces three lines of context for each difference.
-C*n*	Produces *n* lines of context for each difference.

File Manipulation Commands

Continued

-D *def*	Combines *file1* and *file2*, using C preprocessor controls (*#ifdef*).
-e	Creates a script for the **ed** editor to make *file1* the same as *file2*.
-i	Ignores case.
-t	Expands tabs in output to spaces.
-w	Ignores spaces and tabs.

DIROPTIONS

-l	Long format with pagination by **pr**.
-r	Recursively runs **diff** for files in common subdirectories.
-s	Lists identical files.
-S*file*	Starts directory comparisons with *file*, ignoring files alphabetically listed before *file*.

RELATED COMMANDS

bdiff	Compares two files and returns the differences.
comm	Compares two files line by line.
cmp	Compares contents of two files.
diff3	Compares three files.
sdiff	Compares files side by side.

diff3 *options file1 file2 file3*

PURPOSE

Like **diff**, this command compares three different files and reports the differences. It returns one of the following codes:

====	All three files differ.
====1	*file1* is different.
====2	*file2* is different.
====3	*file3* is different.

OPTIONS

-e	Creates an **ed** script that places differences between *file2* and *file3* into *file1*. Not available on all systems.
-E	Creates an **ed** script that places differences between *file2* and *file3* into *file1*, marking lines that differ in all three files with brackets.
-x	Creates an **ed** script that places differences between all three files into another file.
-X	Creates an **ed** script that places differences between all three files into them, marking lines that differ in all three files with brackets. Not available on all systems.
-3	Creates an **ed** script that places differences between *file1* and *file3* into *file1*.

RELATED COMMANDS

bdiff	Compares two files and returns the differences.
cmp	Compares contents of two files.
comm	Compares two files line by line.
diff	Compares two files.
sdiff	Compares files side by side.

File Manipulation
Commands

119

dircmp *options directory1 directory2*

PURPOSE

Compares the contents of two directories and returns information on how the directories differ. The information is given in the form of files found in the first directory, files found in the second directory, and files common to both directories.

OPTIONS

-d	Compares pairs of common files using the **diff** command.
-s	Suppresses information about identical files.
-w_n_	Changes the width of the output line to _n_ characters; the default is 72.

RELATED COMMANDS

bdiff	Compares two files and returns the differences.
diff	Compares two files.
sdiff	Compares files side by side.

egrep *options pattern file(s)*

PURPOSE

Searches for text (referred to as *patterns* or *expressions*) in a file or multiple files, displaying the results of the search. For instance, you could search for the strings *Spacely Sprockets* and *Jetson Enterprises* in multiple files.

Egrep is related to the commands **grep** and **fgrep**. It is considered the most powerful of the three, as it allows for the searching of multiple strings. In addition, **egrep** allows matching from a file containing a series of expressions. It is also considered to be the fastest of the three commands.

EXAMPLE

```
$ egrep "Spacely Sprockets|Jetson Enterprises" *
kevin.memo.1112: This proposal from Spacely Sprockets
erc.doc.193: As a representative of Jetson Enterprises
```

(This searches all the files in the current directory—as indicated by the wildcard asterisk [*]—for the strings *Spacely Sprockets* and *Jetson Enterprises*.)

OPTIONS

-b	Returns block number of matched line.
-c	Returns only the number of matches, without quoting the text.
-e *string*	Used to search for *string* beginning with a hyphen (-).
-f *file*	Takes expressions from file *file*.

Continued

-h	Returns only matched text with no reference to file-names. (Not available on all systems.)
-i	Ignores case.
-l	Returns only filenames containing a match, without quoting the text.
-n	Returns line number of matched text, as well as the text itself.
-v	Returns lines that do *not* match the text.

RELATED COMMANDS

diff	Compares two files.
fgrep	Searches for text in files.
grep	Searches for text in files.
sdiff	Compares files side by side.

fgrep *options pattern file(s)*

PURPOSE

Searches for text (referred to as *patterns*) in a file or multiple files, displaying the results of the search. For instance, you could search for the strings *Spacely Sprockets* and *Jetson Enterprises* in multiple files. **Fgrep** searches only for literal text strings. It will not search for expressions. **Fgrep** is related to the commands **grep** and **egrep**.

EXAMPLE

```
$ fgrep "Spacely Sprockets|Jetson Enterprises" *
kevin.memo.1112: This proposal from Spacely Sprockets is
erc.doc.193: As a representative of Jetson Enterprises
```

(This searches all the files in the current directory—as indicated by the wildcard asterisk [*]—for the strings *Spacely Sprockets* and *Jetson Enterprises*.)

OPTIONS

-b	Returns block number of matched line.
-c	Returns only the number of matches, without quoting the text.
-e *string*	Used to search for *string* beginning with a hyphen (-).
-f *file*	Takes expressions from file *file*.
-h	Returns only matched text with no reference to filenames.
-i	Ignores case.
-l	Returns only filenames containing a match, without quoting the text.

Continued

-n	Returns line number of matched text, as well as the text itself.
-v	Returns lines that do *not* match the text.
-x	Returns a line only if the *string* matches an entire line.

RELATED COMMANDS

diff	Compares two files.
egrep	Searches for text in files.
grep	Searches for text in files.
sdiff	Compares files side by side.

file *options filename*

PURPOSE

Describes file type of given file. If needed, **file** will check
the magic file (**/etc/magic**) for file types.

 **The information returned by file is not always correct.
However, file is best at detecting text files, shell scripts,
WARNING PostScript files, and UNIX commands.**

OPTIONS

-c	Checks the magic file.
-f*list*	Runs the **file** command on the filenames contained in the file **list**.
-h	Ignores symbolic links.
-m*file*	Uses *file* as the magic file, not **/etc/magic**.

find *pathname(s) condition(s)*

PURPOSE

Finds a file. Of course, it's not *quite* that simple—you can enter as many conditions as you want (relating to when the file was created, when it was last accessed, what links are present, and so on, as you'll see when you review the available conditions).

EXAMPLES

```
$ find / -ctime -2 -print
```

(This returns all the files on the entire file system that have been changed fewer than two days ago.)

```
$ file $HOME -name '*memo' -print
```

(This returns all the files in your home directory that end with the string **memo**.)

OPTIONS

-atime *days*   Finds files that were accessed:

                               +*d*   more than *d* days ago.

                               d   exactly *d* days ago.

                               -*d*   fewer than *d* days ago.

-ctime *days*   Finds files that were changed:

                               +*d*   more than *d* days ago.

                               d   exactly *d* days ago.

                               -*d*   fewer than *d* days ago.

Continued

-exec *command* { } \;	Runs UNIX *command* after a file is found.
-follow	Follows symbolic links and the associated directories.
-fstype *type*	Finds files of a specific file *type*.
-group *group*	Finds files belonging to group *group*, which can be a name or ID.
-inum *num*	Finds a file with an inode number of *num*.
-links *links*	Finds files with:
	+*l* more than *l* links.
	l exactly *l* links.
	-*l* fewer than *l* links.
-local	Searches for files on the local file system.
-mtime *days*	Finds files that were modified:
	+*d* more than *d* days ago.
	d exactly *d* days ago.
	-d fewer than *d* days ago.
-name *file*	Finds a file named *file*
-newer *filename*	Returns all files that have been modified more recently than *filename*.
-nogroup	Finds files owned by a group not listed in **/etc/group**.
-nouser	Finds files owned by a user not listed in **/etc/passwd**.
-ok *command* { } \;	Runs UNIX *command* after a file is found, verifying the action with the user.
-perms *nnn*	Matches specified file permissions (such as **rwx**).
-print	Prints the results of the search to the screen. This option is mandatory if you want to see the results of your search.

File Manipulation
Commands

Continued

-size *blocks* [*chars*]	Finds a file that is *blocks* blocks large, or *chars* characters large.
-type *t*	Returns names of files of type *t*. Type *t* can be **b** (block special file), **c** (character special file), **d** (directory), **f** (plain file), **l** (symbolic link), or **p** (pipe).
-user *user*	Matches files belonging to a user, specified by name or ID.
-xdev	Searches for files on the same file system as the specified *pathname*. (Only for BSD systems.)

LOGICAL SELECTORS

-a	and
-o	or
\!	not
\(...\)	group together

grep *options pattern file(s)*

PURPOSE

Searches for text (referred to as *patterns* or *expressions*) in a file or multiple files, displaying the results of the search. For instance, you could search for the string *Spacely Sprockets* in multiple files.

    Grep is related to the commands **fgrep** and **egrep**. Of the three, **grep** supports the fewest options—for instance, **grep** will not accept input from a text file—and is considered to be the slowest.

EXAMPLES

```
$ grep "Spacely Sprockets" *
kevin.memo.1112: This proposal from Spacely Sprockets is
```

(This searches all the files in the current directory—as indicated by the wildcard asterisk [*]—for the string *Spacely Sprockets*.)

OPTIONS

-b	Returns block number of matched line. Not available on all systems.
-c	Returns only the number of matches, without quoting the text.
-h	Returns only matched text with no reference to filenames. Not available on all systems.
-i	Ignores case.
-l	Returns only filenames containing a match, without quoting the text.

File Manipulation Commands

Continued

-n	Returns line number of matched text, as well as the text itself.
-s	Suppresses error messages.
-v	Returns lines that do *not* match the text.

RELATED COMMANDS

diff	Compares two files.
egrep	Searches for text in files.
fgrep	Searches for text in files.
sdiff	Compares files side by side.

head *option file(s)*

PURPOSE

Displays the beginning of a file. The default is 10 lines.

OPTION

-*n*   Specifies the number of lines to display. The default is
                 10 lines.

RELATED COMMAND

tail   Displays end of file.

File Manipulation
Commands

join *options file1 file2*

PURPOSE

Joins together two presorted files that have a common key field. Only lines containing the key field will be joined.

EXAMPLE

```
$ cat workers
Eric      286    erc
Geisha    280    geisha
Kevin     279    kevin

$ cat workers.1
Eric      8      555-6674
Geisha    10     555-4221
Kevin     2      555-1112

join workers workers.1 > workers.2

cat workers.2
Eric      286    erc     8     555-6674
Geisha    280    geisha  10    555-4221
Kevin     279    kevin   2     555-1112
```

OPTIONS

-a*filename*	Lists lines in *filename* that cannot be joined. If *filename* is now specified, unjoinable lines from both files will be listed.
-e *string*	Replaces empty fields in output with *string*.
-j*filename m*	Joins on the *m*th field of file *filename* (or both if *filename* is not specified).

Continued

-o *file.field*	Output contains fields specified by field number *field*.
-t*char*	*Char* will be used as a field separator, instead of the default.

RELATED COMMANDS

awk	Text-processing language.
comm	Compares files line by line.
cut	Cuts fields.
sort	Sorts files.

ln *options originalfile linkfile*

ln *options file(s) directory*

PURPOSE

Links two or more files. In essence, this allows the same file to be accessed under different names. No matter how many names exist, there's still only one file. The **ln** command also creates linked files with the same name in different directories.

You may want to create *symbolic* links, since these links can occur across file systems and are easier to keep track of with the **ls** command.

 Don't reverse the file order with this command, or you can inadvertently trash good files. Remember: *the first file is the original.* The second file names the link. The link then points back at the original file.

EXAMPLES

```
$ ln kevin eric
```

(This creates a link named **eric** to the file **kevin**.)

```
$ ln kevin /usr/users/kevin/misc
```

(This creates a link to **kevin** in **/usr/users/kevin/misc**. The linked file will also be named **kevin**.)

Continued

OPTIONS

-f	Forces linking—that is, does not ask for confirmations.
-n	Does not overwrite an existing file.
-s	Creates a symbolic link.

RELATED COMMANDS

chmod	Changes file-access permissions.
chown	Changse file ownership.
cp	Copies files.
ls	Lists files.
mv	Moves files.

File Manipulation
Commands

ls *options names*

Lists the contents of the specified directory. If no directory is specified, the contents of the current directory are listed.

This is both one of the simplest (conceptually, there's nothing more simple than returning the contents of a directory) and the most complex (witness the presence of 23 options!) commands within the UNIX operating system. Of course, not all of the 23 options are equal; you'll use **-F** and **-l** quite a bit, while chances are you won't find much use for **-u** or **-c**.

EXAMPLES

```
$ ls
data      figures    misc    newdata    personnel
expenses  financials
```

(This returns a listing of the files in the current directory.)

```
$ ls newdata
newdata
```

(This confirms that the file **newdata** is contained in the current directory.)

```
$ ls god
god not found
```

(This searches for a specific file, which is not in the current directory.)

```
$ ls -a
.  ..  .mailrc  .profile  data  financials  misc
   newdata      personnel
```

Continued

(This lists all files, including hidden files, which begin with a period [.].)

OPTIONS

-1	Lists one item per line.
-a	Lists all contents, including hidden files.
-b	Shows invisible characters in octal.
-c	Lists by creation/modification time.
-C	Lists in column (the default).
-d	Lists only the name of the directory, not the contents.
-f	Assumes that *names* are directories, not files.
-F	Flags executable filenames with an asterisk (*), directories with a slash (/), and symbolic links with @.
-g	Lists in long form, omitting the owner of the file.
-i	Lists the inode for each file.
-l	Lists the contents of a directory in long form.
-L	Lists the true files for symbolic links.
-m	Lists the contents across the screen, separated by commas.
-n	Same as **-l**, except it uses numbers instead of names.
-o	Same as **-l**, except the group name is omitted.
-p	Displays a slash (/) at the end of every directory name.
-q	Lists contents with nonprinting characters represented by a question mark (?).
-r	Lists the contents in reverse order.
-R	Recursively lists subdirectories.
-s	Lists file sizes in blocks, instead of the default bytes.
-t	Lists the contents in order of time saved, beginning with the most recent.
-u	Lists files according to the most recent access time.
-x	Lists files in multicolumn format.

File Manipulation Commands

RELATED COMMANDS

chmod	Changes file-access permissions.
chgrp	Changes group.
chown	Changes file ownership.
find	Finds file.
ln	Links files.

mkdir *options directories*

PURPOSE

Creates a new directory or directories.

EXAMPLES

```
$ mkdir stuff
```

(This creates a new directory called **stuff**.)

```
$ mkdir -m 444 stuff
```

(This creates a new directory called **stuff** and sets up file permissions of 444.)

OPTIONS

-m *mode*   Specifies the *mode* of the new directory.

more *options file(s)*

PURPOSE

Displays all or parts of a file one screenful at a time. Type **q** to quit; press space bar to continue.

EXAMPLE

```
$ more bigfile
```

(This displays a file named **bigfile**.)

OPTIONS

-c	Clears the screen before displaying the next page of the file. This can be quicker than watching pages scroll by.
-d	Displays a prompt at the bottom of the screen involving brief instructions.
-f	Wraps text to fit the screen width and judges the page length accordingly.
-l	Ignores formfeeds (^L) at the end of a page.
-r	Displays control characters.
-s	Squeezes; ignores multiple blank lines.
-u	Ignores formatting characteristics like underlined text.
-w	Waits for user input for exiting.
-n	Sets window size by *n* lines.
+num	Starts output at line number *num*.

Continued

OPTIONS DURING FILE VIEWING

f   Goes to next full screen.
n   Displays next file.
p   Displays previous file.
q   Quits.

RELATED COMMAND

pg   Displays file one page at a time.

mv *options sources target*

PURPOSE

Moves a file or multiple files into another directory or to a
new name in the current directory.

EXAMPLES

```
$ mv 1997.report /users/home/misc
```

(This moves the file **1997.report** to the directory named
/users/home/misc.)

```
$ mv 1997.report 1998.report
```

(This renames the file **1997.report** to the new filename
1998.report.)

```
$ mv 1997.report /users/home/misc/1998.report
```

(This saves the file **1997.report** under the name **1998.report**
in the directory **/users/home/misc**.)

```
$ mv -i 1997.report /users/home/misc/1998.report
mv: overwrite 1998.report?
```

(This saves the contents of the file **1997.report** to the new
name **1998.report** in the directory **/users/home/misc**. The
confirmation is required because **1998.report** already exists.)

Continued

OPTIONS

-f   Moves file without checking for confirmation in case
                of an overwrite.
-i   Prompts users if action would overwrite an existing file.

RELATED COMMAND

cp   Copies file.

pack *options file(s)*

PURPOSE

Compresses a file, decreasing its size by up to 50 percent. The original file is replaced by a new file ending in **.z**. For instance, if you were to pack a file named **text**, the original file **text** is erased and a the new file **text.z** appears in the same directory.

Uncompress packed files with the **unpack** command.

OPTIONS

-	Displays information about the compression.
-f	Packs the file even if no disk space is saved.

RELATED COMMANDS

compress	Compresses files.
pcat	Displays contents of packed files.
unpack	Unpacks contents of packed file.

page *options file(s)*

PURPOSE

Displays all or parts of a file. Type **q** to quit; press space bar
to continue.

EXAMPLE

```
$ page bigfile
```

(This displays a file named **bigfile**.)

OPTIONS

-c	Clears the screen before displaying the next page of the file. This can be quicker than watching pages scroll by.
-d	Displays a prompt at the bottom of the screen involving brief instructions.
-f	Wraps text to fit the screen width and judges the page length accordingly.
-l	Ignores formfeeds (^L) at the end of a page.
-r	Displays control characters.
-s	Squeezes; ignores multiple blank lines.
-u	Ignores formatting characteristics like underlined text.
-w	Waits for user input for exiting.
-n	Sets window size by *n* lines.
+num	Starts output at line number *num*.

File Manipulation
Commands

Continued

OPTIONS DURING FILE VIEWING

f	Goes to next full screen.
n	Displays next file.
p	Displays previous file.
q	Quits.

RELATED COMMAND

more	Displays file one page at a time.

pcat *file(s)*

PURPOSE

Displays the contents of a packed file.

RELATED COMMANDS

pack   Compresses a file.
unpack   Uncompresses a file.

File Manipulation
Commands

rm *options file(s)*

PURPOSE

Removes files, provided you're either the owner of the file or have write permission to the directory containing the file (though not necessarily to the file itself). If you don't have write permission to the file itself, you'll be prompted as to whether you really want to delete the file. This command can also be used to delete directories (remember, a directory is merely a file containing information about other files).

Use this command with caution. When a file is removed, it's really gone. Unless you have some
WARNING **undelete utilities at your disposal (for instance, there are versions of the** *Norton Utilities* **for some UNIX variants), you will want to be very careful with this command. We also use the -i option to verify our actions.**

EXAMPLES

```
$ rm textfile
```

(This removes the file named **textfile**.)

```
$ rm textfile?
```

(This removes all files beginning with **textfile** and having a single extra character, like **textfile1**, **textfile2**, and so on.)

```
$ rm -r stuff
```

(This removes the directory named **stuff** and all its contents, including files and subdirectories.)

Continued

OPTIONS

-f   Removes files without verifying action with user.
-i   Removes files after verification from user.
-r   Recursively moves through subdirectories.

RELATED COMMAND

rmdir   Removes directory.

rmdir *options directory*

PURPOSE

Removes a directory. The directory must be empty. To empty a directory that contains other files and directories, use the **rm -r** command.

OPTIONS

-p   Removes the *directory* and any parent directory that is empty as a result of the action.

-s   Ignores error messages.

RELATED COMMAND

rm   Removes file.

sdiff *options file1 file2*

PURPOSE

Compares *file1* with *file2* and reports on the differences as well as on identical lines. Output occurs in four forms:

text text	Lines are identical.
text <	Line exists only in *file1*.
text >	Line exists only in *file2*.
text	*text*	Lines are different.

OPTIONS

-l	Reports only on lines that are identical in *file1*.
-o *outfile*	Sends identical lines to *outfile*.
-s	Does not return identical lines.
-w*n*	Sets line length to *n* (default is 130).

RELATED COMMANDS

bdiff	Compares files.
cmp	Compares two files and tells you if the files are different.
diff	Compares files and reports *all* differing lines.
diff3	Compares three files.

File Manipulation
Commands

split *option file1 file2*

PURPOSE

Splits files into smaller files based on line counts. The default is to create 1,000-line files. This command leaves the original *file1* intact. If *file2* is unnamed, the result files will be named **xaa**, **xab**, **xac**, and so on. If *file2* is named, **aa**, **ab**, **ac** (and so on) will be appended to the end of the specified *file2* name.

If you're looking for more options when splitting a file—after all, using page lengths is a rather inflexible method of dividing files—use the **csplit** command covered elsewhere in this section.

EXAMPLE

```
$ split textfile newtext
```

(This would split **textfile** into smaller files. If **textfile** was 4,500 lines long, **split** would create five files—**newtextaa**, **newtextab**, **newtextac**, **newtextad**, and **nextextae**—with the first four files containing 1,000 lines and the fifth containing 500 lines.)

OPTION

-n   Splits a file into *n*-line segments. (The default is 1,000 lines.)

RELATED COMMAND

csplit   Splits a file.

strings *options file(s)*

PURPOSE

Looks for ASCII strings in binary files. Searches binary or object files for sequences of four or more printable characters, ending with newline or a null character. The **strings** command is useful for identifying binary files, such as object files or word-processor documents made by incompatible software.

OPTIONS

-a	Searches an entire file.
-n *n*	Sets minimum string length (the default is four).

File Manipulation
Commands

153

tail *options file*

PURPOSE

Displays the final 10 lines of a file.

OPTIONS

-f	"Follows" growth of file should changes be made while **tail** command is active. Press **Ctrl-D** to stop the process.
-r	Displays lines in reverse order. Not available on all systems.
-nb	Displays the last n blocks.
+nb	Displays all blocks after block n.
-nc	Displays the last n characters.
+nc	Displays all characters after n.
-nl	Displays the last n lines.
+nl	Displays all lines after line n.

RELATED COMMAND

head	Displays first 10 lines of a file.

tar *options file(s)*

PURPOSE

Archives files to **tar** files, often on backup tapes. (In UNIX, a tape isn't always a tape—in this instance, it may be a tape, hard disk, or diskette.) Specified files can either replace existing files or be appended to existing files. **Tar** is also used to extract archived files from tape.

The usage for the **tar** command differs slightly from the rest of the UNIX command set. Options have two parts: a function option (each command must contain one of these) followed by other options. In addition, the hyphen (-) is not needed before options.

EXAMPLES

```
$ tar cvf /dev/mt0 /usr/users/kevin/memos
```

(This creates a new archive of all files in the directory **/usr/users/kevin/memos** on the device **/dev/mt0**; remember, devices in UNIX are treated as files.)

```
$ tar xvf /dev/mt0 `memo*`
```

(This extracts all files beginning with **memo** from the tape in **/dev/mt0**.)

FUNCTION OPTIONS

c	Creates a new **tar** archive.
r	Appends *files* to the end of the archive.
t	Prints out a table of contents.

Continued

u	Updates archive by appending *files* if not on the tape or if they have been modified.
x	Extracts files from within the **tar** archive.

OPTIONS

b*n*	Sets blocking factor to *n* (default is 1; maximum is 64).
f*dev*	Writes archive to *dev*; default is **/dev/mt0** on many systems.
l	Returns error messages about links that cannot be read.
L	Follows symbolic links.
m	Updates file-modification times to the time of extraction.
o	Changes ownership of extracted files to the current user. This is very useful if the archive was made by another user.
v	Verbose mode: prints out status information.
w	Waits for confirmation.

touch *options date file(s)*

Changes a file's access time and modification time to the current date. If you try to change the date for a file that does not exist, **touch** will create a new file.

This value has more worth than meets the eye. For instance, some systems are set up to delete certain types of files that were created before a particular date and time; the **touch** command makes sure that the timestamp can be easily updated to avoid such deletions. In addition, some commands, such as **find** and **make**, occasionally use a file's timestamp.

Touch uses a *MMddhhmmyy* format for date and time:

MM	month (1–12)
dd	day (1–31)
hh	hour (00–23)
mm	minute (00–59)
yy	year (00–99)

OPTIONS

-a	Updates only the access time.
-c	Does not create a new file if none exists.
-m	Updates only the modification time.

RELATED COMMAND

date	Displays date and time.

File Manipulation
Commands

uncompress   Uncompress File

uncompress *option file(s)*

PURPOSE

Uncompresses a compressed file, which usually has a name ending in **.Z**.

OPTION

-c   Uncompresses without changing original *file(s)*.

RELATED COMMAND

compress   Compresses a file.

unpack *file(s)*

PURPOSE

Unpacks a file shrunk with the **pack** commands. These files usually end with **.z**.

RELATED COMMANDS

pack	Compresses a file.
pcat	Views a packed file.

Text-Processing Commands

These commands cover the various tools needed to edit and format text files.

awk *options 'pattern {action}'files*

PURPOSE

Actually a rudimentary programming language, **awk** is used mainly with text and database files—any structured file, really. It manipulates these files through editing, sorting, and searching.

Awk is an advanced tool that's far too complicated for this introductory work. There's a whole set of specialized commands that are not even listed here, as you'll see from the short example. See the Bibliography for a list of UNIX tutorials that should cover **awk** in some form.

 awk has been superseded somewhat by the nawk (new awk) command, which is also covered in this section. In addition, there's a version in GNU called gawk.

EXAMPLE

```
$ awk '$1 ~ /Geisha/ {print $0}' workers
```

(This command looks in the file **workers** for the string **Geisha** in the first column, which is designated by **$1**, and prints the entire record **$0** to the screen.)

OPTION

-F *sep*   Allows a field separator other than the default space or tab.

RELATED COMMAND

nawk   New version of **awk**.

162

col *options*

PURPOSE

Strips reverse backspaces and other control characters from a file formatted for multiple columns with a text editor like **tbl** or **nroff**. With these characters stripped, files can be displayed on older video screens as well as printed on printers that do not support reverse linefeeds.

This command is not usually used on its own, but as part of a longer command line with the eventual destination of a line printer. It is also handy when used with online manual pages, which are formatted.

EXAMPLE

```
$ cat kevin.report | col | lp
```

(This command sends the file **kevin.report** to **col**, which strips the formatting before printing with the **lp** command.)

OPTIONS

-b	Ignores backspace commands.
-f	Allows half linefeeds.
-p	Prints unknown escape characters as regular characters. (Don't use this option. It usually makes a mess of the final document.)
-x	Does not convert spaces to tabs.

Continued

RELATED COMMANDS

nroff	Text formatter.
tbl	Table editor.
troff	Text formatter.
vi	Text editor

cut *options files*

PURPOSE

Displays a list of columns (specified with the **-c** option) or fields (specified with the **-f** option) from a file or a set of files. A column is exactly what the name describes—a row of characters with the same position on a line—while fields are separated by tabs. Both are referred to by numerals relative to the first column or field on the line.

EXAMPLES

```
$ cut -f1,3 workers > workers_phone
```

(This cuts fields 1 and 3 from the file **workers** and places them into a new file named **workers_phone**.)

```
$ cut -c1,3 workers > workers_phone
```

(This cuts columns 1 and 3 from the file **workers** and places them into a new file named **workers_phone**.)

OPTIONS

-c*list*	Used to cut columns specified by *list* from a file.
-d*character*	Substitutes *character* for the delimiter when the **-f** option is used. If a nonalphabetic character is to be used as the delimiter (such as a space), it must be enclosed in single quote marks.
-f*list*	Used to cut field specified by *list* from a file.
-s	Suppresses (does not return) lines lacking a delimiter; used with the **-f** option.

Continued

RELATED COMMANDS

grep	Finds text in files.
join	Joins lines found in multiple files.
paste	Joins two files in vertical columns.

deroff *options files*

PURPOSE

Removes formatting commands inserted by the **tbl**, **eqn**, **mm**, **nroff**, and **troff** formatting commands.

EXAMPLES

```
$ deroff kevin.report
```

(This removes all formatting commands from the file **kevin.report**.)

```
$ deroff -mm workers
```

(This removes requests from **mm**-formatted files.)

OPTIONS

-ml	Deletes lists from **mm**-formatted files.
-mm	Strips formatting from **mm**-formatted files.
-ms	Strips formatting from **ms**-formatted files.

RELATED COMMANDS

col	Strips control characters.
eqn	Equation editor.
mm	Text formatter.
nroff	Text formatter.
tbl	Table editor.
troff	Text formatter.

ed *options file*

PURPOSE

A rudimentary text editor, superseded by more sophisticated tools like **vi** or **ex**. **Ed** works in two modes—input and command—with very little feedback. It is still used by UNIX in nondirect ways; for instance, the **diff** command calls on the **ed** command.

OPTIONS

—C   Allows for the editing of encrypted files. (This option can be used only in the United States, due to export regulations.)

-p *string*   Substitutes *string* for the standard command prompt (the **ed** default is *).

-s   Suppresses information about file sizes, diagnostic information, and the **!** prompt for shell commands.

-x   Allows for the editing of encrypted files. (This option can be used only in the United States, due to export regulations.)

RELATED COMMANDS

crypt   Encrypts files.
vi   Text editor.

eqn *options files*

PURPOSE

Formats equations created by **troff**, for eventual printing by a printer or typesetting machine. **Eqn** commands are placed into a **troff** file, and then the file is run through **eqn**, with the output usually piped to **troff** and then piped to a printer.

If you are using **nroff** as a text processor, use the **neqn** command.

MACROS

These are to be used within the troff-created files, not on an eqn command line.

N O T E

.EQ   Starts typesetting mathematical characters.
.EN   Stops typesetting mathematical characters.

OPTIONS

-f*font*   Uses font *font*.
-p*n*   Reduces size of superscripts and subscripts by *n* points.
-s*n*   Reduces size of all text by *n* points.
-T*dev*   Formats for the typesetting *dev*, as defined in the TYPESETTER= environment variable.

Continued

RELATED COMMANDS

mm	Text formatter.
neqn	Equation preprocessor used with **nroff**.
nroff	Text formatter.
tbl	Table editor.
troff	Text formatter.
vi	Text editor.

fmt *options files*

PURPOSE

Formats text in a limited fashion—usually only to justify text to the right margin. Text editors like **vi** don't automatically perform this task, so this command is frequently invoked within **vi** (**emacs**, on the other hand, formats text through the **Esc-q** command). In addition, the output of this command is usually piped to a printer command. **fmt** is not available on all systems.

OPTIONS

-c	Does not format the first two lines.
-n	Limits the size of lines to *n* columns wide, instead of the default 72.
-s	Splits long lines, but ignores short lines.
-w*n*	Limits the size of lines to *n* columns wide, instead of the default 72. (This option is not supported in BSD.)

fold *options files*

PURPOSE

Formats text to a specific width, even if the break occurs in the middle of a word.

OPTIONS

-*n*	Limits the size of lines to *n* columns wide, instead of the default 80.
-w*n*	Limits the size of lines to *n* columns wide, instead of the default 80. (This option is not supported in BSD.)

awk options *'pattern {action}' files*

PURPOSE

Actually a rudimentary programming language, **nawk** is used mainly with text and database files—any structured file, really. It manipulates these files through editing, sorting, and searching.

   nawk is an advanced tool that's far too complicated for this introductory work. There's a whole set of specialized commands that are not even listed here. See the Bibliography for a list of UNIX tutorials that should cover **nawk** in some form.

**nawk has superseded the awk command, which is also
covered in this section. In addition, there's a version in
N O T E GNU called gawk.**

neqn *options files*

PURPOSE

Formats equations created by **nroff**, for eventual printing by a printer or typesetting machine. **Neqn** commands are placed into an **nroff** file, and then the file is run through **neqn**, with the output piped to a printer.

If you are using **troff** as a text processor, use the **eqn** command.

MACROS

N O T E

These are to be used within the nroff-created files, not on an neqn command line.

.EQ	Starts typesetting mathematical characters.
.EN	Stops typesetting mathematical characters.

OPTIONS

-ffont	Uses font *font*.
-pn	Reduces size of superscripts and subscripts by *n* points.
-sn	Reduces size of all text by *n* points.
-Tdev	Formats for the typesetting *dev*, as defined in the TYPESETTER= environment variable.

Text-Processing
Commands

Continued

eqn	Equation preprocessor used with **troff**.
mm	Text formatter.
nroff	Text formatter.
tbl	Table editor.
troff	Text formatter.
vi	Text editor.

newform *options file(s)*

PURPOSE

Formats text files by adding and removing characters, changing tab settings, and so on. The **newform** command should be viewed as a down-and-dirty text formatter for those who know precisely what they want; since there's little interactivity between the user and the command, it's easy to make unwanted changes.

OPTIONS

-an	Appends n characters to the end of each line.
-bn	Removes n characters from the beginning of each line.
-c*char*	Uses *char* instead of the default space with the **-a** and **-p** options. (The **-c** option must appear before **-a** or **-p** on the command line.)
-en	Removes n characters from the end of each line.
-i*tabspec*	Sets the tab format defined by *tabspec*. (See the **tabs** command for more information.)
-ln	Sets the default line length in n characters; the default is 72.
-o*tabspec*	Converts tabs to space, as defined by *tabspec*. (See the **tabs** command for more information.)
-pn	Adds n characters to the beginning of each line.
-s	Removes characters before the first tab and places them at the end of the line.

nl *options file*

PURPOSE

Inserts line numbers at the beginning of every line of the file and breaks the file into logical page segments, with the first line of each page numbered *1*.

EXAMPLE

```
$ nl -ba -ht -ft textfile
```

(This formats every line in the file **textfile**, including headers and footers.)

OPTIONS

-b*type*	Numbers lines according to one of four types:
a	All lines.
n	No lines.
p*str*	Lines containing *str*.
t	Only lines containing text.
-d*xy*	Changes *xy* as the delimiter for logical page sections.
-f*type*	Numbers the footers; see the **-b** option for types.
-h*type*	Numbers the headers; see the **-b** option for types.
-i*n*	Increases numbers by *n* increments (default is 1).
-l*n*	Compresses *n* blank lines to one line.
-n*format*	Inserts line numbers in one of three *format*s:
ln	Left justify, no zeroes.
rn	Right justify, no zeroes.
rz	Right justify.

Continued

-p	Does not reset numbering at the beginning of every page.
-s_char_	Inserts _char_ between line numbers and text (default is tab).
-v_n_	Starts page numbering at _n_ (default is 1).
-w_n_	Shows line numbers in _n_ columns (default is 6).

nroff *options file(s)*

PURPOSE

Formats text for printing on a daisywheel or dot-matrix printer. (The related command **troff** prepares files for printing on a laser printer or a typesetter.) The **nroff** command interprets commands already inserted into a text file. For instance, to flush all lines right, you would insert the **.ad r** command within a text file. (This is known as a *dot command*, since it begins with a dot.) When you run the **nroff** command, **nroff** will find the **.ad r** command within the text and format the text accordingly.

Most of the information associated with **nroff** has to do with these commands inserted within files in anticipation of output by **nroff**. For the most part, the same dot commands are used by **troff** and **nroff**, although there's a set of additional files special to **troff**.

There are many formatting options available with **troff** and **nroff**—84 formatting requests alone, plus many registers and characters. We suggest you check your system documentation if you want more information about these commands. Another useful action would be to check out works specifically on **troff** and **nroff**, which are listed in the Bibliography.

EXAMPLES

```
$ nroff textfile | lp
```

(This formats the file **textfile** with **nroff** and sends the results to the line printer.)

Continued

```
$ nroff textfile | more
```

(This formats the file **textfile** and prints the results on the screen one page at a time.)

RELATED COMMAND

troff   Text formatter.

paste *options file(s)*

PURPOSE

Merges files and places them side by side. For instance, the first line of *file1* will be followed by the first line of *file2* in a second column; a tab separates the two columns.

OPTIONS

-	Uses standard input as input (handy when piping output to the command).
d'*char*'	Uses *char* as the delimiter between columns, instead of the default tab. *Char* can be any character, or one of the following:
\n	newline
\t	tab
****	backslash

RELATED COMMANDS

cut	Cuts fields.
join	Joins files.

sort *options files*

PURPOSE

Sorts the lines of named *files,* usually in alphabetical order. Commands like **comm** and **join** require sorted files in order to work.

OPTIONS

-b	Ignores leading spaces and tabs.
-c	Checks if *files* are already sorted. If they are, **sort** does nothing.
-d	Sorts in dictionary order (ignores punctuation).
-f	Ignores case.
-i	Ignores non-ASCII characters.
-m	Merges files that have already been sorted.
-M	Sorts the files assuming the first three characters are months.
-n	Sorts in numeric order.
-o*file*	Stores output in *file*. The default is to send output to standard output.
-r	Reverses sort.
-t*c*	Separates fields with character (default is tab).
-u	Unique output: If merge creates identical lines, uses only the first.
-y*k*	Sets aside *k* kilobytes of memory for the sort. If *k* is not specified, the maximum possible will be allocated.
-z*n*	Provides a maximum of *n* characters per line of input.
+*n***[-***m***]**	Skips *n* fields before sorting, and then sorts through line *m*.

spell *options files*

PURPOSE

Returns incorrectly spelled words in a file. You can also use **spell** to compare spellings against a sorted word file of your own creation. Since it returns only "incorrect" spellings—that is, words not contained in a file of correctly spelled words—**spell** is not as useful as you might think.

EXAMPLE

```
$ spell textfile
```

(This checks the spellings in the file **textfile**.)

```
$ spell +morewords textfile
```

(This checks the spellings in the file **textfile**, against both the main file and the user-created file, **morewords**.)

OPTIONS

-b	Checks for spelling based on British usage.
-l	Checks all included files associated with the target file.
-x	Shows every possible stem of target words.
+_filename_	Creates a sorted file (_filename_) of correctly spelled words.

tabs *tabspec options*

PURPOSE

Sets the tab settings. The default settings are every eighth column (1, 9, 17, and so on). This command supports several preconfigured tab settings for specific languages (see the Options list), or you can set the tabs manually.

TABSPECS

-8	Sets tabs every eighth column (1, 9, 17, and so on). Default.
-a	IBM S/370 assembler (1, 10, 16, 36, 72).
-a2	IBM S/370 assembler (1, 10, 16, 40, 72).
-c	COBOL (1, 8, 12, 16, 20, 55).
-c2	Compact COBOL (1, 6, 10, 14, 49).
-c3	Expanded COBOL (1, 6, 10, 14, 18, 22, 26, 30, 34, 38, 42, 46, 50, 54, 58, 62, 67).
-f	FORTRAN (1, 7, 11, 15, 19, 23).
-p	PL/1 (1, 5, 9, 13, 17, 21, 25, 29, 33, 37, 41, 45, 49, 53, 57, 61).
-s	SNOBOL (1, 10, 55).
-u	UNIVAC 1100 Assembler (1, 12, 20, 44).

OPTIONS

+m*n*	Sets left margin to *n* (default is 10).
-T*type*	Sets terminal *type* (default is TERM).

Table Formatter

tbl *file*

PURPOSE

This preprocessor to **nroff** or **troff** formats tables for eventual
printing. In this day of WYSIWYG, a tool like **tbl** may seem
positively archaic, but it still is useful. With **tbl**, you insert
formatting commands within the text file. When you run **tbl**
on a command line and then pipe the output to **nroff** or **troff**,
the formatting commands are interpreted and you end up
with a file ready either for printing or viewing on the screen.

These formatting commands are rather complicated for
the uninitiated. Be warned that it may take quite a bit of
effort on the part of the beginner to end up with acceptable
output from **tbl**.

EXAMPLES

```
$ tbl textfile | troff |lp
```

(This formats the file **textfile**, first with **tbl** and then with
troff, and sends the subsequent formatted file to the line
printer.)

```
.TS
center, box, tab(%);
cb s s.
Big Ten Standings
_
.T&
1| 1 | 1;
Minnesota%5%1
Michigan%2%3
Wisconsin%1%4
.TE
```

Continued

(This rather rudimentary table would show three columns—headed by Minnesota, Michigan, and Wisconsin—with a bold banner, **Big Ten Standings**.)

FORMATTING OPTIONS

 These are only a few of the major formatting options. Check your documentation or your online manual pages for more information.

.TS	Table Start. This option *must* begin the area formatted by **tbl**.
allbox	Boxes the table and every entry within the table.
box	Boxes the table.
center	Centers the table.
;	End the layout for the table.
c	Center.
l	Flush left.
r	Flush right.
a	Aligns alphabetic entries.
n	Aligns numerical entries.
b	Bold.
i	Italics.
f*fontname*	Font *fontname*.
p*n*	Point size in *n*.
v*n*	Vertical line spacing, *n* points.
.TE	Table End. This option *must* end the area formatting by **tbl**.

tr *options string1 string2*

PURPOSE

Translates characters as part of a global search-and-replace procedure. **Tr** is a quirky command in its syntax, as you'll see in the Examples.

EXAMPLES

```
$ tr '<TAB>' , < textfile
```

(This changes every tab in the file **textfile** to a comma. Note the strange notation for input.)

```
$ cat textfile | tr '[A-Z]' '[a-z]' > newtextfile
```

(This takes input from **textfile**, changes every uppercase letter to its lowercase equivalent, and then saves the output to **newtextfile**.)

OPTIONS

-c	Uses all characters *not* covered by *string1*.
-d	Deletes the characters covered in *string1*.
-s	Squeezes repeated use of a character into a single use.

troff *options file(s)*

PURPOSE

Formats text for printing on a laser printer or a typesetter. (The related command **nroff** prepares files for printing on a daisywheel or dot-matrix printer.) The **troff** command interprets commands already inserted into a text file. For instance, to flush all lines right, you would insert the **.ad r** command within a text file. (This is known as a *dot command*, since it begins with a dot.) When you run the **troff** command, **troff** will find the **.ad r** command within the text and format the text accordingly.

Most of the information associated with **troff** has to do with these commands inserted within files in anticipation of output by **troff**. For the most part, the same dot commands are used by **troff** and **nroff**, although there's a set of additional files special to **troff**.

There are many formatting options available with **troff** and **nroff**—84 formatting requests alone, plus many registers and characters. We suggest you check your system documentation if you want more information about these commands. Another useful action would be to check out works specifically on **troff** and **nroff**, which are listed in the Bibliography.

EXAMPLES

```
$ troff textfile | lp
```

Continued

(This formats the file **textfile** with **troff** and sends the results to the line printer, which **must** be a laser printer or typesetting machine.)

```
$ troff textfile | more
```

(This formats the file **textfile** and prints the results on the screen one page at a time.)

RELATED COMMANDS

eqn	Equation formatter.
nroff	Text formatter.
tbl	Table formatter.

uniq *options file1 file2*

PURPOSE

Identifies and removes duplicate lines from a sorted file. (Uses the **sort** command to sort the file.)

EXAMPLES

```
$ uniq textfile
```

(This removes all duplicate lines in the file **textfile**.)

```
$ uniq textfile text.uniq
```

(This removes all duplicate lines in the file **textfile** and saves them to **text.uniq**.)

OPTIONS

-c	Counts; precedes lines by the number of times they appear.
-d	Deletes all duplicate lines, except the first.
-u	Unique—prints only lines that appear once.
-n	Skips the first *n* lines in a field.
+*n*	Skips the first *n* characters in a field.

RELATED COMMAND

sort	Sorts a file.

vi *options file(s)*

PURPOSE

Vi is a full-screen text editor with many useful options. This summary lists the options but not all the editing commands possible when editing a file. For a list of these commands—and there are indeed *many* of them—either run the **man** command for **vi** or check out a book that contains a reference section on **vi** commands.

The **vi** editor runs mainly in two modes: command mode and insert mode. In insert mode, you enter text. In command mode, you modify text or issue commands. (We list some of the more useful commands here, but many more are available.) Press **Escape** to exit input mode and return to command mode.

For more information on **vi**, we suggest picking up a more complete UNIX tutorial, such as *Teach Yourself UNIX* (MIS:Press, 1992). While **vi** isn't exactly the most complex command, it does require a little background and a little explanation of the underlying concepts.

EXAMPLES

```
$ vi
```

(This begins a **vi** text-editing session.)

```
$ vi textfile
```

(This starts **vi** with the file **textfile** loaded for editing.)

Continued

OPTIONS

-c *command*	Starts **vi** and runs *command*.
-C	Edits an encrypted file (see the **crypt** command for more information).
-l	Runs **vi** in LISP mode for editing LISP files.
-L	Lists the files that were saved despite a system failure.
-r*file*	Recovers *file* after a system crash.
-R	Runs in read-only mode, which means that files cannot be changed.
-w*n*	Sets window size to *n* lines of text.
-x	Creates an encrypted file (see the **crypt** command for more information).
+	Starts **vi** on the last line of the file.
+*line*	Starts **vi** with *line* as the top line in the window.

vi COMMANDS

/*pattern*	Searches for *pattern*, going forward.
/*pattern*	Searches for *pattern*, going backward.
*n*G	Goes to line number *n*.
h	Same as the left arrow key. Useful for keyboards lacking arrow keys.
j	Same as the down arrow key. Useful for keyboards lacking arrow keys.
k	Same as the up arrow key. Useful for keyboards lacking arrow keys.
l	Same as the right arrow key. Useful for keyboards lacking arrow keys.
Ctrl-F	Goes forward one page.

Continued

Ctrl-B	Goes backward one page.
ZZ	Saves file and exits.
:w	Saves file.
:q	Quits without saving file.
:wq	Saves file and quits the command.
:n	Goes to next file on the command line.
:n!	Goes to next file on the command line, even if you haven't saved the current file.
:q!	Quits without saving file.
dw	Deletes word.
dd	Deletes line.
i	Enters insert mode.
a	Enters append mode, inserting after current position.
Esc	Exits inserti or append mode

RELATED COMMANDS

crypt	Encrypts files.
mm	Text formatter.
nroff	Text formatter.
tbl	Table editor.
troff	Text formatter.

wc *options file(s)*

PURPOSE

Counts the number of words, characters, and lines in a text file or files. The terse output presents the number of lines, followed by the words and characters.

OPTIONS

-c	Prints only the number of characters.
-l	Prints only the number of lines.
-w	Prints only the number of words.

Printing Commands

These commands cover the actual printing commands as well as the commands that prepare files for printing.

banner *string*

PURPOSE

Displays up to 10 characters in large letters using asterisks
(*) or number signs (#), depending on your system.

EXAMPLE

```
$ banner kevin
```

creates the following output:

```
#    #   ######  #    #   #    #       #
#  #    #        #    #   #    ##      #
###     ####     #    #   #    # #     #
# #     #        #    #   #    #  #  #
#   #   #         #  #    #    #     ##
#    #   ######    ##     #    #      #
```

196

cancel · Cancel Printing

cancel *options printer*

PURPOSE

This cancels pending printer jobs initiated with the **lp** command. You can either specify the job ID or the printer to be canceled. (Privileged users can use the command to cancel jobs created by a specific user.)

OPTIONS

job-id   Cancels the specific *job-id*.

-u *user*   Cancels the print requests made by a specific *user*.

Printing
Commands

lp *options files*

PURPOSE

Sends a print request to a printer. This command can be used to print multiple files with one request. On some systems, you may need to use the **lpr** command instead.

Not all of the following options are available on every system due to configuration differences. Check with your system administrator to see which options are supported.

OPTIONS

-c	Copies the file to a print spooler before sending the request.
-d *printer*	Specifies a printer other than the default printer.
-d any	Used with the **-f** and **-s** options to find any printer that supports a form or character set specified by *name*.
-f *name*	Prints on the form *name*; used in conjunction with the **-d any** option.
-H *action*	Prints according to one of these actions:

         hold: Suspends current or pending print job.

         immediate: Prints immediately after current job is completed.

         resume: Resumes suspended print job.

-m	Sends a mail message to the user when the file is printed.
-n *num*	Prints *num* number of copies (the default is 1).
-o *option*	Sets printer-specific options:

         cpi=*n*:   Prints *n* characters per inch; **pica**, **elite**, or **compressed** can be used instead of *n*.

Continued

length=*n*	Page length, specified in inches (*ni*), lines (*n*), or centimeters (*nc*).
lpi=*n*	Prints *n* lines per inch.
nobanner	Does not print the banner page.
nofilebreak	Does not print form feed between files.
stty=*list*:	Returns a *list* of options for **stty**.
width=*n*	Page width, specified in inches (*ni*), lines (*n*), or centimeters (*nc*).
-P *list*	Prints the page numbers specified by *list*.
-q *level*	Sets a priority *level* for the print job (lowest is 39).
-s	Suppresses messages from **lp**.
-S *name*	Uses the character set or print wheel *name*.
-t *title*	Prints *title* banner on every page.
-T *type*	Prints on a printer that supports *type*. (See your system administrator about which *types* are supported.)
-w	Sends a terminal message to the user when the file is printed.
-y *list*	Prints according to locally defined nodes, contained in *list*.

RELATED COMMANDS

cancel	Cancels print requests.
lpsched	Turns on the print spooler.
lpshut	Turns off the print spooler.
lpstat	Shows printer status.

lpshut

PURPOSE

Turns on a print spooler. A print spooler stores print requests in memory, allocating them to printers. This allows several print requests to be stored in RAM simultaneously, freeing the users who originate the print requests to go on with their work. This command can be run from a prompt but is more effectively used when placed in the **rc** file, where it will be launched when the system starts. Normally, system adminstrators run **lpsched**.

OPTIONS

None.

RELATED COMMAND

lpshut   Turns off the print spooler.

lpsched

PURPOSE

Turns off the print spooler.

OPTIONS

None.

RELATED COMMAND

lpsched   Turns on the print spooler.

lpstat *options*

PURPOSE

Returns the status of print requests, either individually or systemwide.

OPTIONS

-a [*list*]	Tells whether the *list* of printers or class names is accepting print requests.
-c [*list*]	Displays the names of all class names and printers contained in *list*.
-d	Shows the name of the default destination printer.
-D	Used with **-p** to show a description of the printer.
-f [*list*]	Displays the forms supported by the system in *list*. The **-l** option returns a description of these forms.
-o [*list*]	Returns the status of output requests by printer name, class name, and request ID.
-p [*list*]	Shows the status of all printers in *list*.
-r	Shows whether the print scheduler (or print spooler, as controlled by **lpsched**) is on or off.
-R	Shows the position of a job in the queue.
-s	Summarizes print status.
-S [*list*]	Displays character sets or print wheel supported in *list*.
-t	Shows all status information.

Continued

-u [*list*]   Shows the status of requests made by users on *list*.
                      In this instance, *list* refers to:
                      user: *User* on the local machine.
                      all: All users.
                      host!use: *user* on machine *host*.
                      host!all: All users on *host*.
                      all!*user*: *User* not on local machine.
                      all!all: All users.
-v [*list*]   Displays pathnames of devices for all printers (or
                      printers listed in *list*.)

RELATED COMMANDS

cancel   Cancels print requests.
lp   Prints files.
lpsched   Turns on the print spooler.

Printing
Commands

pr *options file(s)*

PURPOSE

Prepares a file for printing to standard output. If you want to print to the default printer, for instance, you'd pipe the output to **lp**. Each printed page contains a header, which includes a page number, filename, date, and time. There are many options for formatting the file, such as multiple columns.

EXAMPLE

```
$ pr textfile | lp
```

(This prepares the file **textfile** for printing and then sends the result to the default line printer.)

```
$ pr textfile
```

(This prepares the file **textfile** for printing and displays the results on the screen.)

OPTIONS

-a	Prints multiple columns in rows across the page.
-d	Double-spaces the text.
-ecn	Sets tabs (as specified by c) to every nth position (default is 8).
-f	Separates pages by form feeds, not blank lines.
-F	Folds input lines to avoid truncation.
-h *text*	Prints the header *text* at the beginning of the output.

Continued

-icn	Replaces white space with c (default is tab) every nth position (default is 8).
-ln	Sets the page length to n (default is 66).
-m	Merges input files, placing each in its own column.
-ncn	Numbers lines with numbers n digits in length (default is 5), separated from the text by c (default is a tab).
-on	Offsets each line by n spaces.
-p	Pauses between pages; handy when reading off of a screen.
-r	Suppresses messages about files that can't be found.
-sc	Separates columns with c (default is tab).
-t	Does not print page header.
-wc	Sets the page width to c (default is 72).
+num	Begins printing at page num.
-num	Prints output with num columns.

Printing Commands

RELATED COMMANDS

cat	Concatenates files.
join	Joins files.
paste	Concatenates files horizontally.

Internet/Communication Commands

These commands work when you're on the Internet or trying to connect to other UNIX and non-UNIX systems.

ct *options -speed -w -x system*

PURPOSE

This command allows you to call another terminal and log on a remote UNIX system via modem or direct line.

EXAMPLES

```
$ ct -s9600 5555555
```

(This calls the telephone number 555-5555 at 9600 bps.)

```
$ ct -s9600 nicollet
```

(This calls the remote system **nicollet** at 9600 bps, as long as **nicollet** appears on a list of systems supported by the **uuname** command.)

OPTIONS

-h	Prevents hang-ups.
-v	Outputs status to standard output.
-s*speed*	Sets bits-per-second rate.
-w*min*	Waits *min* minutes for remote system to answer.
-x*n*	Debugging mode at *n* level.
system	Phone number or system name.

RELATED COMMANDS

cu	Calls up another system.
uuname	Listing of UNIX-to-UNIX system names.

cu options system

PURPOSE

Calls up another UNIX system or terminal, or a non-UNIX bulletin-board service or online service, via modem or direct line. Other computer systems have a separate telecommunications package. In UNIX, telecommunications capabilities are built into the operating system.

EXAMPLES

```
$ cu -s9600 5555555
```

(This calls the telephone number 555-5555 at 9600 bps.)

```
$ cu -s9600 nicollet
```

(This calls the remote system **nicollet** at 9600 bps, as long as **nicollet** appears on a list of systems supported by the **uuname** command.)

OPTIONS

-bn	Sets bit length to 7 or 8.
-cname	Searches the **UUCP Device** file for *name*.
-d	Sets diagnostics mode.
-e	Sets even parity. (Opposite of **-o**.)
-h	Sets half-duplex.
-lport	Specifies port for communications.
-n	Prompts the user for a telephone number.
-o	Sets odd parity. (Opposite of **-e**.)

Continued

-s*rate*	Sets bits-per-second rate (300, 1200, 2400, 9600, et al.).
-t	Calls an ASCII terminal.

ONLINE COMMANDS

These commands are to be run after a connection to the remote system.

~!*command*	Runs *command* on the local system.
~$*command*	Runs *command* on the local system and then sends the output to the remote system.
~%cd *directory*	Changes to directory *directory* on local system.
~%put *file*	Copies *file* from the local system to the remote system.
~$take *file*	Takes *file* from the remote system and places it on the local system.
~!	Exits **cu**.
~.	Disconnects the telephone link between the two systems.
~?	Displays a listing of all online commands.

RELATED COMMANDS

ct	Calls terminal.
uuname	Listing of UNIX-to-UNIX system names.

This command is covered in its own chapter. See Chapter 8, "FTP Commands," for more details.

Internet Communication Commands

logname

PURPOSE

Returns your login name, or more precisely, the value of the **$LOGNAME** environment variable.

OPTIONS

None.

RELATED COMMAND

login   Login a system.

mailx *options users*

PURPOSE

Used to send mail to other users and to receive mail. This command supersedes the **mail** command found in many older versions of UNIX. Files can be attached to **mailx**-created messages. See the **uuencode** command for more information.

Some system administrators also install other mail front ends in their systems, such as **elm**, **mailtool**, or **dtmail**. Check with your system administrator to see if you should be using **mailx** or another mail program.

Internet
Communication
Commands

EXAMPLES

```
$ mailx erc
Subject:
```

(This sends a mail message to **erc**. After the **mailx** command is given, the system prompts for a subject and a message text. After you're finished editing text, press **Ctrl-D** to end the input.)

```
$ mailx erc < memo
```

(This sends the contents of the file **memo** to **erc** in the form of a mail message.)

Continued

OPTIONS

-d	Sets debugging mode.
-e	Checks for mail without printing it.
-f *file*	Stores mail in file named *file* (default is **mbox**).
-F	Stores mail in file named after the first recipient of the message.
-h *n*	Sets number of network hops to *n*.
-i	Ignores interrupts.
-I	Saves newsgroup and article IDs; used in conjunction with **-f**.
-n	Ignores startup **mailx.rc** file.
-N	Ignores mail headers.
-r *address*	Specifies a return *address* for your mail.
-s *subject*	Enters *subject* in the "Subject:" field, avoiding the prompt.
-T *file*	Records message and article IDs in *file*.
-U	Converts a **uucp** address to an Internet address.
-V	Version number.

RELATED COMMANDS

uucp	UNIX-to-UNIX copy.
uuencode	Encodes files for transmission with **mailx**.

mesg *options*

PURPOSE

Grants or denies permission to other users to send you messages via the **write** or **talk** commands.

EXAMPLES

```
$ mesg -y
```

(This allows messages.)

```
$ mesg -n
```

(This forbids messages.)

OPTIONS

-n   Forbids messages.
-y   Allows messages.

RELATED COMMANDS

talk   Talks with another user via the network.
write   Sends a message to a user.

Internet
Communication
Commands

notify *options*

PURPOSE

Notifies a user when new mail arrives. This command is not available on all systems. Some systems have a **check-mail** command instead.

OPTIONS

-m *file*   Saves mail messages to *file* when the **-y** option is enabled.

-n   Disables mail notification.

-y   Enables mail notification.

RELATED COMMAND

mailx   Sends and receives mail.

rcp *options source target*

PURPOSE ,

Copies files to and from remote systems. This command
assumes you have permissions in the target directory.
Generally, this command is used in conjunction with the
rlogin command: First you log on a remote machine with
rlogin and then transfer files with the **rcp** command. To
name remote files, use *hostname:filename.*

EXAMPLES

```
$ rcp nicollet:/u/erc/reports/report.1997 report.copy
```

(This copies **nicollet:/u/erc/reports/report.1997** on remote
machine **nicollet** to **report.copy** on the local machine.)

```
$ rcp report.1997 attila:/users/kevin
```

(This copies local file **attila:/users/kevin** to the **/users/kevin**
directory on remote machine **attila**.)

OPTIONS

-p	Preserves the permissions of the source file.
-r	Recursively copies each subdirectory.

RELATED COMMANDS

ftp	File-transfer protocol.
mailx	Sends and receives mail.
rlogin	Remote login.
uucp	UNIX-to-UNIX copy.

Internet
Communication
Commands

rlogin *options hostname*

PURPOSE

Logs in to a remote system. A list of the available *hostnames* is stored in the **/etc/hosts/.rhosts** file. If your *local* hostname is listed in the **.rhosts** file in your home directory on the *remote* machine, you won't have to enter a password. Your local computing session is suspended while you're logged on a remote machine. Any UNIX commands you use will be run on the remote machine. When you're finished on the remote system, use an **exit** command or press **Ctrl-D** to end the connection.

OPTIONS

-8	Uses 8-bit data (default is 7 bits).
-e *c*	Uses *c* as the default escape character (default is ~).
-l *username*	Remotely login under the new *username*, instead of the name on your local host.

RELATED COMMANDS

ftp	File-transfer protocol.
mailx	Sends and receives mail.
rcp	Remote copy.
uucp	UNIX-to-UNIX copy.

rsh *options hostname command*

PURPOSE

Starts a remote shell on a remote machine, executing a command on the remote machine.

On some systems, **rsh** refers to the *restricted* shell. The remote shell is then called **remsh**.

OPTIONS

-l *user*   Logs in *user* to the remote machine.

-n   Diverts input to **/dev/null**, which can be useful when troubleshooting.

sum *option filename(s)*

PURPOSE

Computes and prints a checksum and block count for a specified *file*. While this command isn't specifically geared toward communications, it's used most often when communicating files back and forth to remote systems, ensuring that the transferred files are the same size on both ends.

The BSD version of this command differs slightly. To match the results of a BSD-generated **sum** command, use the **-r** option.

OPTION

-r   Uses alternative algorithm to compute checksum and
                    size; matches BSD version of command.

RELATED COMMAND

wc   Word count.

talk *username[@hostname] terminal*

PURPOSE

Carries on a conversation with another user on the network. The command splits your screen into two areas: The top half contains your typing, while the bottom contains messages from the other user. Press **Ctrl-D** to exit.

The **write** command is similar, except that **write** is geared for single messages and not for an ongoing dialog.

OPTIONS

user	Other user, obviously.
hostname	The *hostname* of the machine the *user* is logged on, if the user isn't logged on to your local machine.
terminal	Specifies a *tty* should the *user* be logged on more than one terminal.

RELATED COMMANDS

mesg	Blocks communications.
write	Writes a message to another terminal.

Internet
Communication
Commands

221

telnet *system port*

PURPOSE

Logs in to a remote system using the TELNET protocol. After you login the remote system, your prompt will change to the **telnet** prompt (telnet>), from which you can enter TELNET commands. **telnet** also supports an input mode, in which you can enter commands directly on the remote system. Use the escape character (**Ctrl-]** or ^, depending on your system setup) to switch between the two modes.

OPTIONS

system	Name of remote system or its network address.
port	Optional port identification.

ONLINE COMMANDS

close	Ends remote session and exits the program.
display *values*	Displays **set** and **toggle** values.
mode *mode*	Changes mode to **character** or **line**.
open *system*	Opens connection to *system*.
quit	Ends remote session and exits the program.
send *chars*	Sends special characters to the remote system:

ao	Abort output.
ayt	Are you there?
brk	Break.
ec	Erase character.
el	Erase line.
escape	Escape.
ga	Go ahead.
ip	Interrupt process.

222

Continued

	nop	No operation.
	synch	Synch.
	?	Help for **send** command.
set *value*	Sets one of the following values:	
	echo	Local echo on or off.
	eof	End of file.
	erase	Erase character.
	escape	New Escape character.
	flushoutput	Flush output.
	interrupt	Interrupt process.
	kill	Erase line.
	quit	Break.
status	Displays status.	
toggle *values*	Changes one of the following values:	
	autoflush	Send **interrupt** or **quit** to remote system.
	autosynch	Synch after **interrupt** or **quit**.
	crmod	Convert **CR** to **CR LF**.
	debug	Debugging mode.
	localchars	Convert local commands to remote control.
	netdata	Convert hexadecimal display of network data.
	options	Protocol processing.
	?	Display settings.
z	Suspends **telnet**.	
?	Displays summary of online commands.	

RELATED COMMAND

rlogin	Remote login.

uucp *options source! destination! file(s)*

PURPOSE

Copies files to and from remote UNIX system. The *file(s)* may also be entire directories. Normally the destination is a public, secure directory named **uucppublic**; this prevents unwanted visitors from roaming around a UNIX system where they are not wanted.

EXAMPLE

```
$ uucp textfile harmar!/usr/users/geisha/uucppublic
```

(This copies the file **textfile** to the machine named **harmar** in the directory **/usr/users/geisha/uucpublic**.)

OPTIONS

-c	Copies the actual file, not a copy from the spool file.
-C	Copies to a spooling file before sending on to the destination machine.
-d	Creates a directory to match the directory sent from the source machine. (This is the default.)
-f	Does not create a directory to match the directory sent from the source machine.
-gp	Sets job priority to *p*.
-j	Prints job number.
-m	Notifies sender via mail when transfer is complete.
-n *user*	Notifies *user* via mail when transfer is complete.
-r	Queues the *file(s)*, but doesn't send them.
-sfile	Sends the transfer status to *file* (instead of to user, as specified by **-m**.)
-xn	Debugs at level *n*; lowest is 1, highest is 9.

Continued

RELATED COMMANDS

ftp	File-transfer protocol.
mailx	Sends and receive mail.
rlogin	Remote login.
uulog	Logs **uucp** traffic.
uustat	Returns status of **uucp**.
uux	Executes command on remote system.

Internet
Communication
Commands

uudecode *file*

PURPOSE

Reads a file converted by **uuencode** and restores it to original form.

RELATED COMMAND

uuencode   Encodes file for **mailx**.

uuencode   Encode Binary File

unencode *filename* **| mailx** *username*

PURPOSE

Converts a binary *filename* to an encoded form that can be
sent with the **mailx** command. This encoded file is in ASCII
form.

RELATED COMMANDS

mailx   Sends mail.
uudecode   Decodes file encoded by **uuencode**.

uulog *options*

PURPOSE

Keeps a log of **uucp** file transfers to and from a specified system.

OPTIONS

-**f***system* Applies the **-tail** command to display the most recent file transfers.

-**s***system* Displays all actions on the specified *system*.

RELATED COMMAND

uucp   UNIX-to-UNIX copy.

uuname *options*

PURPOSE

Lists the UNIX system that can be accessed with UNIX
communications tools like **mailx** or **uucp**.

Do not confuse uuname with uname.

OPTIONS

-c   Prints system names that can be accessed with the **cu**
            command.

-l   Prints the name of the local system.

RELATED COMMANDS

cu   Calls up another system.

mailx   Sends and receives mail.

uucp   UNIX-to-UNIX copy.

uustat *options*

PURPOSE

Returns information about the current status of **uucp** commands. It can also be used to cancel **uucp** requests. Not all of the following options are available on all systems.

OPTIONS

-a	Reports on the status for all jobs.
-c	Reports the average time spent in queue.
-d*n*	Reports average for the last *n* minutes (default is last hour).
-j	Reports the total number of jobs.
-k*id*	Kills job *id*; you must own the job.
-m	Shows what systems can be accessed.
-n	Shows standard output but not standard error.
-p	Runs **ps -flp** on current processes.
-q	Reports on the jobs queued for all systems.
-r*n*	Runs **touch** on its job *n*.
-s*system*	Reports the status of jobs on *system*.
-S*type*	Reports the status of jobs of *type*:

	c	completed
	i	interrupted
	q	queued
	r	running

-t*system*	Reports the average transfer rate on *system*.
-u*user*	Reports on the jobs started with *user*.

RELATED COMMANDS

cu	Calls up another system.
mailx	Sends and receives mail.
uucp	UNIX-to-UNIX copy.

230

uux *options system! command*

PURPOSE

Runs a UNIX command on a remote UNIX system. It also copies files to and from other UNIX systems. A listing of permissible commands can often be found on a remote system in **etc/uucp/permissions**.

OPTIONS

-a*user*	Notifies *user* when command is completed.
-b	Returns the input if an error interrupts the *command*.
-c	Copies the actual file, not a copy from the spool file.
-C	Copies to a spooling file before sending on to the destination machine.
-g*p*	Sets job priority to *p*.
-j	Prints **uux** job number.
-n	Does not send mail if the *command* fails.
-p	Uses standard input for *command*.
-r	Queues the *file(s)*, but doesn't send them.
-s*file*	Sends the transfer status to *file* (instead of to user, as specified by **-m**.)
-x*n*	Debugs at level *n*; lowest is 1, highest is 9.
-z	Notifies user who initiated command when it is completed.

RELATED COMMANDS

mailx	Sends and receives mail.
rlogin	Remote login.
uucp	UNIX-to-UNIX copy.

vacation *options*

PURPOSE

Returns a mail message to the originator indicating that you're on vacation. This lets people know you are not ignoring them. **vacation** is not available on all systems, and versions vary among systems.

OPTIONS

-F *user*	Forwards mail to *user* when *mailfile* is unavailable.
-l *logfile*	Logs names of senders in *logfile* (default is **$HOME/.maillog**).
-m *mailfile*	Saves messages in *mailfile* (default is **$HOME/.mailfile**).
-M *file*	Uses *file* as the message sent to mail originators (default is **/usr/lib/mail/std_vac_msg**).

wall

PURPOSE

Sends a message to all users. After sending the message, you can end input with **Ctrl-D**. This command is most often used by system administrators to warn users about a pending system shutdown.

EXAMPLE

```
$ wall
WARNING: System will be shut down in 5 minutes.
```

(This sends a warning message to all users logged on the system.)

Internet
Communication
Commands

write *user tty*

PURPOSE

Sends a text message to another user. Press **Ctrl-D** to exit.

EXAMPLE

```
$ write eric
Hi Eric
Ctrl-D
```

(This sends the message "Hi Eric" to user **eric**.)

Graphics Commands

These commands are used on a graphic display. Many of the commands have an *x* in their names because they come from the X Window System, which provides the base technology for graphics on UNIX. Other commands start with *dt*, which is short for desktop and indicates that a command is part of the Common Desktop Environment, or CDE, available on many commercial versions of UNIX. An alternative to the CDE interface is called Open Look, available on Sun and Linux systems. On Sun Solaris, Open Look is part of Sun's X Window System package called OpenWindows.

Many of the CDE, Open Look, and base X Window System commands overlap. To edit a text file, for example, you can choose **dtpad** (on CDE systems), **textedit** (on Open Look systems), or **xedit** (on most X systems including CDE and Open Look systems). Because of this, your system will not have all of these commands.

All of these commands have something in common: a long list of toolkit options. Depending on which toolkit they were created with, the commands in this section accept *xview* or *xt* options. (There's a lot of overlap between the toolkit options, as you can see.) These options control how the window is displayed.

Xview OPTIONS

-background *red green blue* — Sets background color to *red green blue* values.

-background *color* — Uses *color* for window background.

-bg *color* — Uses *color* for window background.

-display *host:disp_num* — Connects to *disp_num* numbered X server (almost always 0) on a given *host*.

-fg *color* — Uses *color* for window foreground.

-fn *fontname* — Uses given font.

-font *fontname* — Uses given font.

-foreground_color *red green blue* — Sets foreground color to *red green blue* values.

-foreground *color* — Uses *color* for window foreground.

-geometry *WidthxHeight+x+y* — Sets window size and position.

-geometry *WidthxHeight* — Sets window size.

-geometry *+x+y* — Sets position of window's upper-left corner.

-height *rows* — Sets height of base window, in rows.

-position *x y* — Sets location of upper-left corner of window, in pixels.

-reverse — Reverses foreground and background colors.

-rv — Reverses foreground and background colors.

-size *width height* — Sets base window size, in pixels to *width* x *height*.

-Wb *red green blue* — Sets background color to *red green blue* values.

-Wf *red green blue* — Sets foreground color to *red green blue* values.

-WG *WidthxHeight+x+y* — Sets window size and position.

-WG *WidthxHeight* — Sets window size.

-WG *+x+y* — Sets position of window's upper-left corner.

-Wh *rows* — Sets height of base window, in rows.

-Wi — Starts window as an icon.

-width *columns*	Sets width of base window, in columns.
-Wp *x y*	Sets location of upper-left corner of window, in pixels.
-Wr *host:disp_num*	Connects to *disp_num* numbered X server (almostalways 0) on given *host*.
-Ws *width height*	Sets base window size, in pixels to *width* x *height*.
-Wt *fontname*	Uses given font.
-Ww *columns*	Sets width of base window, in columns.

XT OPTIONS

-background *color*	Uses *color* for window background.
-bd *color*	Uses *color* for window border.
-bg *color*	Uses *color* for window background.
-bordercolor *color*	Uses *color* for window border.
-borderwidth *num_pixels*	Sets border to *num_pixels* wide.
-bw *num_pixels*	Sets border to *num_pixels* wide.
-display *host:disp_num*	Connects to *disp_num* numbered X server (almost always 0) on given *host*.
-fg *color*	Uses *color* for window foreground.
-fn *fontname*	Uses given font.
-font *fontname*	Uses given font.
-foreground *color*	Uses *color* for window foreground.
-geometry *WidthxHeight+x+y*	Sets window size and position.
-geometry *WidthxHeight*	Sets window size.
-geometry *+x+y*	Sets position of window's upper-left corner.
-iconic	Starts window as an icon.
-reverse	Reverses foreground and background colors.
-rv	Reverses foreground and background colors.

bdftopcf *options font_file.bdf*

PURPOSE

Converts font from bitmap distribution format (BDF) to portable compiled format (PCF). Use it when you get an X font and want to install it on your system, because most X fonts are distributed in BDF format.

EXAMPLES

```
bdftopcf times.bdf > times.pcf
```

(Converts BDF font file **times.bdf** and redirects output to file **times.pcf**.)

```
bdftopcf -o times.pcf times.bdf
```

(Converts BDF font file **times.bdf**, writing output to PCF file **times.pcf**.)

OPTIONS

-l	Sets the font bit order to least significant bit first.
-L	Sets the font byte order to least significant byte first.
-m	Sets the font bit order to most significant bit first.
-M	Sets the font byte order to most significant byte first.
-o *filename*	Sends output to *filename*.
-t	Converts to a fixed-width font.

RELATED COMMAND

mkfontdir	Adds new font.

bitmap *options*
bitmap *options filename*
bitmap *options filename basename*

PURPOSE

Monochrome bitmap editor. The *filename* is the name to store the bitmap. The *basename* is used for the bitmap name inside the file.

EXAMPLES

```
bitmap -size 48x32 mybitmap.xbm
```

(Creates a new bitmap 48 pixels wide and 32 pixels high to be stored in the file **mybitmap.xbm**.)

```
bitmap -fr red -hl yellow +dashed
```

(Uses solid grid lines, in red and yellow, for selected areas.)

OPTIONS

-axes	Turns on an X across the bitmap for positioning.
+axes	Turns off an X across the bitmap for positioning.
-background *color*	Uses *color* for window background.
-bd *color*	Uses *color* for window border.
-bg *color*	Uses *color* for window background.
-bordercolor *color*	Uses *color* for window border.
-borderwidth *num_pixels*	Sets border to *num_pixels* wide.
-bw *num_pixels*	Sets border to *num_pixels* wide.
-dashed	Turns on dashed lines for grid, the default.

Graphic
Commands

239

Continued

+dashed	Turns off dashed lines for grid. Use this if performance is slow.
-display *host:disp_num*	Connects to *disp_num* numbered X server (almost always 0) on given *host*.
-fg *color*	Uses *color* for window foreground.
-fn *fontname*	Uses given font.
-font *fontname*	Uses given font.
-foreground *color*	Uses *color* for window foreground.
-fr *color*	Uses *color* for the frame and grid lines.
-geometry *WidthxHeight* **+x+y**	Sets window size and position.
-geometry *WidthxHeight*	Sets window size.
-geometry **+x+y**	Sets position of window's upper-left corner.
-grid	Turns on grid lines.
+grid	Turns off grid lines.
-hl *color*	Uses *color* for highlighting.
-iconic	Starts window as an icon.
-proportional	Forces all dots to be square.
+proportional	Used with **-sh** and **-sw** to allow for non-square dots.
-reverse	Reverses foreground and background colors.
-rv	Reverses foreground and background colors.
-size *WidthxHeight*	Sets size, in pixels, of bitmap to edit.
-sh *size*	Sets height of each square (for each dot) to *size* pixels.
-sw *size*	Sets width of each square (for each dot) to *size* pixels.

RELATED COMMANDS

dticon	Desktop icon bitmap editor.
iconedit	Open Look icon bitmap editor.

calctool *options*

PURPOSE

Provides a calculator in the Open Look environment.

OPTIONS

-2	Uses a two-dimensional look, the default for monochrome systems.
-3	Uses a three-dimensional look, the default for color systems.
-a *accuracy_value*	Controls number of decimal digits displayed, from 0 to 9. Defaults to 2.
-l	Starts up with a "left-handed" display.
-r	Starts up with a "right-handed" display, the default.
-v	Lists version number of all available options.
-Wn	Starts clock with no title bar.
+Wn	Starts clock with a title bar.

RELATED COMMANDS

dtcalc	Common Desktop Environment calculator.
xcalc	X calculator.

Graphic
Commands

clock *options*

PURPOSE

Displays current time in a window; Open Look program.

OPTIONS

-12	Displays 12-hour time in the digital clock.
-24	Displays 24-hour time in the digital clock.
-analog	Displays a clock with hands.
-digital	Displays a digital clock.
+date	Shows the current date.
-date	Does not show the current date.
-TZ *timezone*	Displays time from *timezone* rather than your normal timezone.
-v	Lists version number of all available options.
-Wn	Starts clock with no title bar.
+Wn	Starts clock with a title bar.

RELATED COMMANDS

oclock	Displays current time in a round window.
xclock	Displays current time.

242

cm *options*

PURPOSE

Appointment calendar in the Open Look environment. Normally started from Open Look window manager.

OPTIONS

-background *red green blue*	Sets background color to *red green blue* values.
-background *color*	Uses *color* for window background.
-bg *color*	Uses *color* for window background.
-c *calendar*	Sets name of default calendar.
-display *host:disp_num*	Connects to *disp_num* numbered X server (almost always 0) on given *host*.
-fg *color*	Uses *color* for window foreground.
-fn *fontname*	Uses given font.
-font *fontname*	Uses given font.
-foreground_color *red green blue*	Sets foreground color to *red green blue* values.
-foreground *color*	Uses *color* for window foreground.
-geometry *Width*x*Height+x+y*	Sets window size and position.
-geometry *Width*x*Height*	Sets window size.
-geometry *+x+y*	Sets position of window's upper-left corner.
-height *rows*	Sets height of base window, in rows.
-i 2	Displays current month when iconified.
-i 3	Displays current date when iconified.
-position *x y*	Sets location of upper-left corner of window, in pixels.
-reverse	Reverses foreground and background colors.

Continued

-rv	Reverses foreground and background colors.
-size *width height*	Sets base window size, in pixels to *width* x *height*.
-Wb *red green blue*	Sets background color to *red green blue* values.
-Wf *red green blue*	Sets foreground color to *red green blue* values.
-WG *WidthxHeight+x+y*	Sets window size and position.
-WG *WidthxHeight*	Sets window size.
-WG *+x+y*	Sets position of window's upper-left corner.
-Wh *rows*	Sets height of base window, in rows.
-Wi	Starts window as an icon.
-width *columns*	Sets width of base window, in columns.
-Wp *x y*	Sets location of upper-left corner of window, in pixels.
-Wr *host:disp_num*	Connects to *disp_num* numbered X server (almost always 0) on given *host*.
-Ws *width height*	Sets base window size, in pixels to *width* x *height*.
-Wt *fontname*	Uses given font.
-Ww *columns*	Sets width of base window, in columns.

RELATED COMMAND

dtcm	Desktop calendar manager.

cmdtool *options*
cmdtool *options program args*

PURPOSE

Provides a shell terminal window, allowing you to enter UNIX commands. You can run multiple **cmdtool** windows on your display and copy and paste between them. Inside the window, **cmdtool** runs your UNIX shell, which is specified in the SHELL environment variable. Or, you can specify a program and arguments on the command line.

OPTIONS

program args	Runs *program* with arguments.
-background *red green blue*	Sets background color to *red green blue* values.
-background *color*	Uses *color* for window background.
-bg *color*	Uses *color* for window background.
-C	Captures system console messages and displays in window.
-display *host:disp_num*	Connects to *disp_num* numbered X server (almost always 0) on given *host*.
-fg *color*	Uses *color* for window foreground.
-fn *fontname*	Uses given font.
-font *fontname*	Uses given font.
-foreground_color *red green blue*	Sets foreground color to *red green blue* values.
-foreground *color*	Uses *color* for window foreground.
-geometry *WidthxHeight* +x+y	Sets window size and position.
-geometry *WidthxHeight*	Sets window size.
-geometry +x+y	Sets position of window's upper-left corner.
-height *rows*	Sets height of base window, in rows.

245

Continued

-l *command*	Passes *command* to the shell.
-position *x y*	Sets location of upper-left corner of window, in pixels.
-reverse	Reverses foreground and background colors.
-rv	Reverses foreground and background colors.
-size *width height*	Sets base window size, in pixels to *width* x *height*.
-Wb *red green blue*	Sets background color to *red green blue* values.
-Wf *red green blue*	Sets foreground color to *red green blue* values.
-WG *Width***x***Height***+x+y*	Sets window size and position.
-WG *Width***x***Height*	Sets window size.
-WG +x+y	Sets position of window's upper-left corner.
-Wh *rows*	Sets height of base window, in rows.
-Wi	Starts window as an icon.
-width *columns*	Sets width of base window, in columns.
-Wp *x y*	Sets location of upper-left corner of window, in pixels.
-Wr *host:disp_num*	Connects to *disp_num* numbered X server (almost always 0) on given *host*.
-Ws *width height*	Sets base window size, in pixels to *width* x *height*.
-Wt *fontname*	Uses given font.
-Ww *columns*	Sets width of base window, in columns.

RELATED COMMANDS

shelltool	Open Look terminal.
dtterm	Common Desktop Environment terminal.
xterm	X terminal.

dtcalc *options*

PURPOSE

Common Desktop Environment calculator utility.

EXAMPLES

```
$ dtcalc -b binary -no_menu_bar
```

(Starts calculator in binary mode with no menubar.)

```
$ dtcalc -notation engineering -m financial
```

(Starts calculator with engineering notation but in financial mode.)

OPTIONS

-?	Prints a usage message.
-a *accuracy_value*	Controls number of decimal digits displayed, from 0 to 9. Defaults to 2.
-b *binary*	Starts with binary numeric base.
-b *octal*	Starts with octal numeric base.
-b *decimal*	Starts with decimal numeric base, the default.
-b *hexadecimal*	Starts with hexadecimal numeric base.
-background *color*	Uses *color* for window background.
-bd *color*	Uses *color* for window border.
-bg *color*	Uses *color* for window background.
-bordercolor *color*	Uses *color* for window border.
-borderwidth *num_pixels*	Sets border to *num_pixels* wide.

Continued

-bw *num_pixels*	Sets border to *num_pixels* wide.
-display *host:disp_num*	Connects to *disp_num* numbered X server (almost always 0) on given *host*.
-fg *color*	Uses *color* for window foreground.
-fn *fontname*	Uses given font for text.
-font *fontname*	Uses given font.
-foreground *color*	Uses *color* for window foreground.
-geometry *WidthxHeight+x+y*	Sets window size and position.
-geometry *WidthxHeight*	Sets window size.
-geometry *+x+y*	Sets position of window's upper-left corner.
-iconic	Starts window as an icon.
-m *financial*	Starts in financial mode.
-m *logical*	Starts in logical mode.
-m *scientific*	Starts in scientific mode, the default.
-no_menu_bar	Displays calculator without a menubar.
-notation *engineering*	Uses engineering notation.
-notation *fixed*	Uses fixed notation, the default.
-notation *scientific*	Uses scientific notation.
-reverse	Reverses foreground and background colors.
-rv	Reverses foreground and background colors.
-trig *degrees*	Uses degrees for trigonometric data in scientific mode.
-trig *gradients*	Uses gradients for trigonometric data in scientific mode.
-trig *radians*	Uses radians for trigonometric data in scientific mode.

RELATED COMMAND

xcalc	Calculator.

dtcm *options*

PURPOSE

Manages a calendar of things to do and remember—part of the Common Desktop Environment.

EXAMPLE

```
dtcm -v day
```

(Starts calendar in day view, showing today.)

OPTIONS

-c *calendar*	Names the *calendar* to display. Your default calendar is $USER@$HOST, for example *erc@eric.com*.
-p *printer*	Names the *printer* to use. Defaults to system printer.
-v *day*	Starts with day view.
-v *week*	Starts with week view.
-v *month*	Starts with month view.
-v *year*	Starts with year view.

RELATED COMMAND

cm	Open Look calendar manager.

Graphic
Commands

dtfile *options*

PURPOSE

Manages files in the Common Desktop Environment. The easiest way to launch this program is from the CDE front panel.

EXAMPLES

```
dtfile -view attributes
```

(Views files by name and small icons signifying attributes.)

```
dtfile -dir /home/erc
```

(Starts in directory **/home/erc**.)

OPTIONS

-dir *folder*	Displays a window for named *folder* (directory).
-folder *folder*	Displays a window for named *folder* (directory).
-grid off	Displays file icons where they get placed.
-grid on	Displays file icons in a grid pattern.
-noview	Runs in server mode with no windows until an application requests windows.
-order alphabetical	Displays files in alphabetical order.
-order file_type	Groups files by type.
-order date	Displays files in order of last modified dates.
-order size	Displays files in order of size.
-tree off	Displays files in a single folder.

Continued

-tree on	Displays files in tree mode rather than in a single folder.
-view no_icon	Displays files by name.
-view large_icon	Displays files by name and large icon.
-view small_icon	Displays files by name and small icon.
-view attributes	Displays files by name and small attribute icon.

RELATED COMMAND

filemgr	Open Look File Manager.

dthelpview *options*

PURPOSE

Views online help in the Common Desktop Environment. It an also display online manual pages. You start **dthelpview** either with one of the command-line options listed below or by simply clicking on the help icon in the CDE front panel.

EXAMPLES

```
dthelpview -helpVolume 1
```

(Tries to display bogus help volume 1. You can then click on the *Index* button to display an index of all available volumes.)

```
dthelpview -manPage cal
```

(Displays online manual entry for the **cal** command.)

```
dthelpview -man
```

(Prompts you for an online manual page. Does not provide a list of available pages, alas.)

```
dthelpview -file larry1
```

(Displays ASCII file **larry1**.)

Continued

OPTIONS

-file *filename*	Displays given ASCII file.
-helpVolume *volume*	Displays CDE help volume.
-manPage *man_page*	Displays named online manual page (entry).
-man	Prompts for an online manual page to display.

RELATED COMMANDS

man	Prints online manual.
xman	Views online manuals.

**Graphic
Commands**

253

dticon *options*

PURPOSE

Common Desktop Environment icon bitmap editor. **dticon** supports XPM (X Pixmap) color and XBM (X Bitmap) monochrome images formats. It can also capture areas of the screen.

EXAMPLES

```
dticon -x 32x48
```

(Creates a new bitmap for editing, 32 pixels wide and 48 pixels high.)

```
dticon -f recycle.xbm
```

(Edits existing bitmap file **recycle.xbm**.)

OPTIONS

-f *filename*   Edits given *filename*.
-x *WidthxHeight* Specifies size of icon to create, in pixels.

RELATED COMMANDS

bitmap   Bitmap editor.

dtksh *options*

PURPOSE

Provides an extended Korn shell, **ksh**, with windowing commands. Your scripts can create windows and access the CDE help system. For most usage, though, **dtksh** acts like **ksh**, the Korn shell, one of UNIX's many command-line interfaces. See Chapter 7, "Shell Commands and Variables," for more information on the Korn shell.

dtlp *options*

dtlp *options filename*

PURPOSE

Presents a print dialog window in which you can specify all the printing options, then it prints a file. As the name suggests, **dtlp** acts as a front-end to **lp**, described earlier in this chapter. Located in **/usr/dt/bin/dtlp**.

EXAMPLES

```
dtlp -b "This is MY file so there"
```

(Displays the print dialog with the printing title banner set to "This is MY file so there".)

```
dtlp -n 5 -d bigprinter -s secret_report
```

(Silently prints 5 copies of the file **secret_report** on the printer named *bigprinter*. Does not display a print dialog.)

OPTIONS

-a	Formats file with the **man** command.
-b *banner*	Sets text of the banner page to banner.
-d *printer_name*	Names the printer.
-e	Erases file after printing it.
-h	Prints out a help message.
-m *print_command*	Replaces the printer command, **lp**, with *print_command*.

Continued

-n *copy_count*	Sets number of copies to *copy_count*.
-o *other_options*	Sets extra options to pass to the print command, which defaults to **lp**.
-r	Format file with the **pr -f** command before printing it.
-s	Prints the file silently, without displaying the print dialog.
-u *user_filename*	Sets name of file to appear in the print dialog.
-v	Prints out verbose messages as **dtlp** works.
-w	Sends raw file data to printer, without special handling for tabs, backspaces, formfeeds and other binary characters.

RELATED COMMANDS

lp	Prints files.
man	Shows online manual.

Graphic
Commands

257

dtmail *options*

PURPOSE

This Common Desktop Environment email program allows you to send and receive messages. Located in **/usr/dt/bin/ dtmail**.

EXAMPLES

```
dtmail -f ~/Mail/my_mailbox
```

(Starts **dtmail** and uses the file **~/Mail/my_mailbox** as the mailbox file.)

```
dtmail -c
```

(Starts **dtmail** with just the compose window.)

```
dtmail
```

(Starts **dtmail** with the normal message window.)

OPTIONS

-a *filename*	Brings up compose window with *filename* included as an attachment.
-a *filename1 ... filenameN*	Brings up compose window with all listed files included as attachments.
-background *color*	Uses *color* for window background.
-bd *color*	Uses *color* for window border.
-bg *color*	Uses *color* for window background.
-bordercolor *color*	Uses *color* for window border.
-borderwidth *num_pixels*	Sets border to *num_pixels* wide.

Continued

-bw *num_pixels*	Sets border to *num_pixels* wide.
-c	Starts **dtmail** with an empty compose window.
-display *host:disp_num*	Connects to *disp_num* numbered X server (almost always 0) on given *host*.
-f *mailfile*	Uses *mailfile* instead of your default mailbox file (named by the MAIL environment variable).
-fg *color*	Uses *color* for window foreground.
-fn *fontname*	Uses given font.
-font *fontname*	Uses given font.
-foreground *color*	Uses *color* for window foreground.
-geometry *WidthxHeight+x+y*	Sets window size and position.
-geometry *WidthxHeight*	Sets window size.
-geometry *+x+y*	Sets position of window's upper-left corner.
-h	Prints summary of command-line options.
-iconic	Starts window as an icon.
-reverse	Reverses foreground and background colors.
-rv	Reverses foreground and background colors.

RELATED COMMANDS

mail	Sends and receives email.
mailx	Sends and receives email.

Graphic Commands

dtpad *options*

dtpad *options filename*

PURPOSE

GUI text editor for the Common Desktop Environment.

EXAMPLES

```
dtpad filename
```

(Starts **dtpad** editing file **filename**.)

```
dtpad -saveOnClose -statusLine filename
```

(Starts **dtpad** editing file **filename**; saves files when closed and shows a status line.)

OPTIONS

-background *color*	Uses *color* for window background.
-bd *color*	Uses *color* for window border.
-bg *color*	Uses *color* for window background.
-bordercolor *color*	Uses *color* for window border.
-borderwidth *num_pixels*	Sets border to *num_pixels* wide.
-bw *num_pixels*	Sets border to *num_pixels* wide.
-display *host:disp_num*	Connects to *disp_num* numbered X server (almost always 0) on given *host*.
-exitOnLastClose	Quits when last file is closed.
-fg *color*	Uses *color* for window foreground.

Continued

-fn *fontname*	Uses given font.
-font *fontname*	Uses given font.
-foreground *color*	Uses *color* for window fore-ground.
-geometry *WidthxHeight+x+y*	Sets window size and position.
-geometry *WidthxHeight*	Sets window size.
-geometry *+x+y*	Sets position of window's upper-left corner.
-iconic	Starts window as an icon.
-missingFileWarning	Alerts you when a filename cannot be found.
-noReadOnlyWarning	Doesn't alert you when a file is read only.
-noNameChange	Doesn't change default filename when you use *Save As* on the *File* menu. The default option is to change the name.
-reverse	Reverses foreground and background colors.
-rv	Reverses foreground and background colors.
-saveOnClose	Automatically saves files when closed.
-statusLine	Displays status line at bottom of window.
-viewOnly	Doesn't allow you to change files.
-workspaceList *workspace_list*	Displays window in given work-space (or workspaces).
-wrapToFit	Wraps text to fit. Default is not to wrap.

RELATED COMMANDS

textedit	Open Look text editor.
xedit	Text editor.

Graphic
Commands

dtstyle

PURPOSE

Calls up Common Desktop Environment style manager, from which you can select fonts and colors for all Common Desktop Environment applications.

OPTIONS

None.

dtterm *options*

dtterm *-e program options*

PURPOSE

Opens a shell terminal window, allowing you to enter UNIX commands. You can run multiple **dtterm** windows on your display and copy and paste between them. Inside the window, **dtterm** runs your UNIX shell, which is specified in the SHELL environment variable.

EXAMPLES

```
dtterm &
```

(Runs **dtterm** in the background.)

```
dtterm -e rlogin eric
```

(Launches **dtterm** and executes **rlogin** to remotely login to machine *eric* rather than launching your shell.)

OPTIONS

-background *color*	Uses *color* for window background.
-bd *color*	Uses *color* for window border.
-bg *color*	Uses *color* for window background.
-bordercolor *color*	Uses *color* for window border.
-borderwidth *num_pixels*	Sets border to *num_pixels* wide.
-bw *num_pixels*	Sets border to *num_pixels* wide.

Graphic
Commands

Continued

-C	Captures output sent to **/dev/console** and displays in this window.
-display *host:disp_num*	Connects to *disp_num* numbered X server (almost always 0) on given *host*.
-e *program*	Executes *program* and passes all following options to *program*.
-fg *color*	Uses *color* for window foreground.
-fn *fontname*	Uses given font.
-font *fontname*	Uses given font.
-foreground *color*	Uses *color* for window foreground.
-geometry *WidthxHeight+x+y*	Sets window size and position.
-geometry *WidthxHeight*	Sets window size.
-geometry *+x+y*	Sets position of window's upper-left corner.
-iconic	Starts window as an icon.
-reverse	Reverses foreground and background colors.
-ls	Starts a login shell (reads **.profile** or **.login**.)
-map	Maps (deiconifies) window if it is iconified and new output arrives.
-name *progname*	Uses *progname* as program's name; default for icon name.
-rv	Reverses foreground and background colors.
-title *titlestring*	Sets window title.
-usage	Displays a usage message explaining the options.

RELATED COMMANDS

xterm	Terminal window.
cmdtool	Open Look terminal window.
shelltool	Open Look terminal window.

dtwm *options*

PURPOSE

Controls placement and size of windows on the screen. It is normally started automatically when you login Common Desktop Environment systems.

EXAMPLE

```
dtwm -display eric:0
```

(Starts **dtwm** as the window manager for display eric:0, that is, the first X server on machine *eric*.)

OPTIONS

-display *host:disp_num*	Connects to *disp_num* numbered X server (almost always 0) on given *host*.
-name *name*	Uses name for finding resources, rather than the default resource name of *Dtwm*.

Graphic Commands

RELATED COMMANDS

twm	Tab window manager.
mwm	Motif window manager.
olwm	Open Look window manager.

265

filemgr *options*

PURPOSE

The Open Look file manager program allows you to view, copy, move, rename, and delete files. It is normally started from the Open Look window manager, **olwm**.

OPTIONS

-a	Checks both file and directory modification times, limiting performance.
-background *red green blue*	Sets background color to *red green blue* values.
-background *color*	Uses *color* for window background.
-bg *color*	Uses *color* for window background.
-C	Doesn't use system for typing files. With **-C**, **filemgr** only understands generic documents, folders, and programs.
-c	Displays in columns, not rows.
-d *directory*	Starts in given *directory*.
-display *host:disp_num*	Connects to *disp_num* numbered X server (almost always 0) on given *host*.
-fg *color*	Uses *color* for window foreground.
-fn *fontname*	Uses given font.
-font *fontname*	Uses given font.
-foreground_color *red green blue*	Sets foreground color to *red green blue* values.
-foreground *color*	Uses *color* for window foreground.
-geometry *Width*x*Height+x+y*	Sets window size and position.
-geometry *Width*x*Height*	Sets window size.
-geometry *+x+y*	Sets position of window's upper-left corner.
-height *rows*	Sets height of base window, in rows.

Continued

-i *secs*	Checks directories (and files with **-a**) for modification every *secs* seconds.
-position *x y*	Sets location of upper-left corner of window, in pixels.
-r	Displays in rows, not columns; the default.
-reverse	Reverses foreground and background colors.
-rv	Reverses foreground and background colors.
-size *width height*	Sets base window size, in pixels to *width* x *height*.
-Wb *red green blue*	Sets background color to *red green blue* values.
-Wf *red green blue*	Sets foreground color to *red green blue* values.
-WG *WidthxHeight+x+y*	Sets window size and position.
-WG *WidthxHeight*	Sets window size.
-WG *+x+y*	Sets position of window's upper-left corner.
-Wh *rows*	Sets height of base window, in rows.
-Wi	Starts window as an icon.
-width *columns*	Sets width of base window, in columns.
-Wp *x y*	Sets location of upper-left corner of window, in pixels.
-Wr *host:disp_num*	Connects to *disp_num* numbered X server (almost always 0) on given *host*.
-Ws *width height*	Sets base window size, in pixels to *width* x *height*.
-Wt *fontname*	Uses given font.
-Ww *columns*	Sets width of base window, in columns.

RELATED COMMAND

dtfile	Desktop File Manager.

Graphic Commands

fsinfo *options*

PURPOSE

Prints out information about font servers, which provide scaled fonts.

OPTIONS

-server *host:port*   Returns information on the given font server, located on the given host, using the given network port number, instead of the font server named in the FONTSERVER environment variable.

RELATED COMMANDS

fslsfonts   Lists fonts provided by a font server.

xfs   Font server.

fslsfonts *options*

PURPOSE

Lists the available fonts that a font server provides and can scale.

OPTIONS

-1	Prints output using only one column.
-C	Prints output in multiple columns.
-fn *pattern*	Lists fonts that match the *pattern*. * and ? wild-cards are allowed.
-l	Lists some attributes of font as well as names.
-ll	Lists font properties in addition to output from **-l** option.
-m	Prints minimum and maximum bounds of each font.
-n *columns*	Sets number of columns to *columns*.
-server *host:port*	Returns information on the given font server, located on the given host, using the given network port number, instead of the font server named in the FONTSERVER environment variable.
-u	Doesn't sort output.
-w *width*	Sets total width of output to *width* characters.

RELATED COMMANDS

fsinfo	Prints information on font server.
xfs	Font server.

Graphic
Commands

269

fstobdf -*server server* -*fn fontname*

fstobdf -*fn fontname*

PURPOSE

Converts a font from the font server into the bitmap distribution format, or BDF. You can have the font server scale a font and then convert that font to BDF format for installing on another system.

OPTIONS

-fn *fontname*   Names font to extract to BDF format.

-server *host:port*   Returns information on the given font server, located on the given host, using the given network port number, instead of the font server named in the FONTSERVER environment variable.

RELATED COMMANDS

fsinfo   Prints information on font server.

fslsfonts   Lists fonts provided by a font server.

xfs   Font server.

ghostview *options filename*

PURPOSE

Displays PostScript documents in a window. Not available on all systems.

EXAMPLES

```
ghostview budget.ps
```

(Displays PostScript document **budget.ps**.)

OPTIONS

-10x14	Sets standard page size to 10 x 14 inches.
-a3	Uses A3 paper size.
-a4	Uses A4 paper size.
-a5	Uses A5 paper size.
-b4	Uses B4 paper size.
-b5	Uses B5 paper size.
-center	Centers page within viewport.
-color	Uses a color palette.
-date	Shows PostScript %%Date comment.
-dpi *dpi*	Sets resolution to *dpi* dots per inch.
-executive	Sets standard page size to 7.5 x 10 inches.
-folio	Sets standard page size to 10 x 14 inches.
-grayscale	Uses a grayscale palette.
-landscape	Sets default orientation to Landscape.
-ledger	Sets standard page size to 17 x 11 inches.
-legal	Sets standard page size to 8.5 x 14 inches.
-letter	Sets standard page size to 8.5 x 11 inches.
-locator	Displays locator.

Graphic Commands

271

Continued

-magstep	Sets default magnification step. Defaults to 0.
-monochrome	Displays only in monochrome.
-ncdwm	Workaround if window appears extremely small.
-nocenter	Doesn't center page within viewport.
-nodate	Doesn't show PostScript %%Date comment.
-nolocator	Doesn't display locator.
-noncdwm	Turns off workaround for extremely small windows.
-noopenwindows	Turns off workaround for Sun OpenWindows systems.
-noquiet	Prints informational messages.
-notitle	Doesn't show PostScript %%Title comment.
-openwindows	Workaround for errors on Sun OpenWindows systems.
-portrait	Sets default orientation to Portrait.
-quiet	Doesn't print informational messages.
-resolution *dpi*	Sets resolution to *dpi* dots per inch.
-seascape	Rotates orientation 90 degrees counter-clockwise.
-statement	Sets standard page size to 5.5 x 8.5 inches.
-tabloid	Sets standard page size to 11 x 17 inches.
-title	Shows PostScript %%Title comment.
-upsidedown	Sets orientation to upside down.
-xdpi *dpi*	Sets horizontal resolution of window to *dpi* dots per inch.
-ydpi *dpi*	Sets vertical resolution of window to *dpi* dots per inch.

RELATED COMMAND

xdvi	Previews DVI Documents.

iconedit *filename options*
iconedit *options*

PURPOSE

Edits Open Look icons and cursors.

EXAMPLE

```
iconedit myicon.icon
```

(Starts **iconedit** with icon file **myicon.icon**. If the file exists, you'll see that icon in the window. Otherwise, it will create a new icon named **myicon.icon**.)

OPTIONS

-background *red green blue*	Sets background color to *red green blue* values.
-background *color*	Uses *color* for window background.
-bg *color*	Uses *color* for window background.
-display *host:disp_num*	Connects to *disp_num* numbered X server (almost always 0) on given *host*.
-fg *color*	Uses *color* for window foreground.
-fn *fontname*	Uses given font.
-font *fontname*	Uses given font.
-foreground_color *red green blue*	Sets foreground color to *red green blue* values.
-foreground *color*	Uses *color* for window foreground.
-geometry *Widthx Height+x+y*	Sets window size and position.
-geometry *WidthxHeight*	Sets window size.
-geometry *+x+y*	Sets position of window's upper-left corner.

Graphic
Commands

273

Continued

-height *rows*	Sets height of base window, in rows.
-position *x y*	Sets location of upper-left corner of window, in pixels.
-reverse	Reverses foreground and background colors.
-rv	Reverses foreground and background colors.
-size *width height*	Sets base window size, in pixels to *width* x *height*.
-Wb *red green blue*	Sets background color to *red green blue* values.
-Wf *red green blue*	Sets foreground color to *red green blue* values.
-WG *WidthxHeight+x+y*	Sets window size and position.
-WG *WidthxHeight*	Sets window size.
-WG *+x+y*	Sets position of window's upper-left corner.
-Wh *rows*	Sets height of base window, in rows.
-Wi	Starts window as an icon.
-width *columns*	Sets width of base window, in columns.
-Wp *x y*	Sets location of upper-left corner of window, in pixels.
-Wr *host:disp_num*	Connects to *disp_num* numbered X server (almost always 0) on given *host*.
-Ws *width height*	Sets base window size, in pixels to *width* x *height*.
-Wt *fontname*	Uses given font.
-Ww *columns*	Sets width of base window, in columns.

RELATED COMMANDS

bitmap	Bitmap editor.
dticon	Desktop icon bitmap editor.

mailtool *options*

PURPOSE

This Open Look email program allows you to send and receive messages. It is located in **/usr/openwin/bin/mailtool**.

OPTIONS

-background *red green blue*	Sets background color to *red green blue* values.
-background *color*	Uses *color* for window background.
-bg *color*	Uses *color* for window background.
-display *host:disp_num*	Connects to *disp_num* numbered X server (almost always 0) on given *host*.
-fg *color*	Uses *color* for window foreground.
-fn *fontname*	Uses given font.
-font *fontname*	Uses given font.
-foreground_color *red green blue*	Sets foreground color to *red green blue* values.
-foreground *color*	Uses *color* for window foreground.
-geometry *WidthxHeight+x+y*	Sets window size and position.
-geometry *WidthxHeight*	Sets window size.
-geometry *+x+y*	Sets position of window's upper-left corner.
-height *rows*	Sets height of base window, in rows.
-Mx	Works in expert mode. Won't ask you to confirm deleting messages.
-Mi *interval*	Checks for new mail every *interval* seconds.

Graphic Commands

Continued

-Mf *mailfile*	Uses *mailfile* instead of the default in-box, in **/var/mail/***username*.
-position *x y*	Sets location of upper-left corner of window, in pixels.
-reverse	Reverses foreground and background colors.
-rv	Reverses foreground and background colors.
-size *width height*	Sets base window size, in pixels to *width* x *height*.
-v	Prints **mailtool** version number.
-Wb *red green blue*	Sets background color to *red green blue* values.
-Wf *red green blue*	Sets foreground color to *red green blue* values.
-WG *WidthxHeight+x+y*	Sets window size and position.
-WG *WidthxHeight*	Sets window size.
-WG *+x+y*	Sets position of window's upper-left corner.
-Wh *rows*	Sets height of base window, in rows.
-Wi	Starts window as an icon.
-width *columns*	Sets width of base window, in columns.
-Wp *x y*	Sets location of upper-left corner of window, in pixels.
-Wr *host:disp_num*	Connects to *disp_num* numbered X server (almost always 0) on given *host*.
-Ws *width height*	Sets base window size, in pixels to *width* x *height*.
-Wt *fontname*	Uses given font.
-Ww *columns*	Sets width of base window, in columns.

RELATED COMMAND

dtmail	Common Desktop Environment email program.

mkfontdir

mkfontdir *directory*

PURPOSE

Scans all the font files in a directory and creates the
fonts.dir file with a listing of these fonts. You must run
mkfontdir after you have copied a new font file into a font
directory, usually under **/usr/lib/X11/fonts**. You normally
have to be the root user to run **mkfontdir**, because the font
directories usually have restrictive permissions.

OPTIONS

The only option is a directory name. If one is omitted,
mkfontdir works in the current directory.

RELATED COMMAND

xlsfonts   Lists installed fonts.

**Graphic
Commands**

mwm *options*

PURPOSE

Controls the placement and size of windows on the screen. Usually, a window manager gets started when you begin an X session. **mwm** displays window titlebars with a Motif look and feel.

OPTION

-display *host:disp_num*   Connects to *disp_num* numbered X server (almost always 0) on given *host*.

RELATED COMMANDS

dtwm	Common Desktop Environment window manager.
olwm	Open Look window manager.
twm	Tab window manager.

oclock *options*

PURPOSE

Displays the time in a round window.

EXAMPLES

```
oclock -hour red -jewel gold
```

(Starts a round clock with a red hour hand and a gold "jewel".)

```
oclock -transparent
```

(Starts a round clock with a transparent background.)

OPTIONS

-bd *color*	Uses *color* for window border.
-bg *color*	Uses *color* for window background.
-bw *num_pixels*	Sets border to *num_pixels* wide.
-display *host:disp_num*	Connects to *disp_num* numbered X server (almost always 0) on given *host*.
-fg *color*	Uses *color* for window foreground.
-geometry *WidthxHeight+x+y*	Sets window size and position.
-geometry *WidthxHeight*	Sets window size.
-geometry *+x+y*	Sets position of window's upper-left corner.
-hour *color*	Uses *color* for hour hand.
-jewel *color*	Uses *color* for clock jewel.
-minute *color*	Uses *color* for minute hand.

Graphic
Commands

Continued

-noshape	Creates a rectangular clock.
-shape	Creates a rounded clock.
-transparent	Creates a clock with a transparent background.

RELATED COMMANDS

clock	Open Look clock.
xclock	X clock.

olwm *options*

PURPOSE

Controls the placement and size of all windows on the display and provides window title bars with an Open Look appearance.

EXAMPLES

```
olwm -follow -3d
```

(Starts **olwm** with keyboard focus following the mouse—rather than having to click to type—and with a three-dimensional look.)

```
olwm -2d -fg maroon
```

(Starts **olwm** with a foreground color of maroon and with a two-dimensional look.)

OPTIONS

-2d	Uses a two-dimensional look, the default for monochrome systems.
-3d	Uses a three-dimensional look, the default for color systems.
-background *color*	Uses *color* for window background.
-bd *color*	Uses *color* for window border.
-bg *color*	Uses *color* for window background.
-bordercolor *color*	Uses *color* for window border.
-c	You must click a mouse button in a window to make it active.
-click	You must click a mouse button in a window to make it active.

Graphic
Commands

Continued

-display *host:disp_num*	Connects to *disp_num* numbered X server (almost always 0) on given *host.*
-f	As you move the mouse, windows underneath the mouse become active.
-follow	As you move the mouse, windows underneath the mouse become active.
-fn *font_name*	Sets titlebar font to *font_name.*
-fn *fontname*	Uses given font.
-font *fontname*	Uses given font.
-fg *color*	Sets titlebar foreground color to *color.*
-foreground *color*	Uses *color* for window foreground.
-name *name*	Uses *name* for finding resources, rather than the default **olwm**.

RELATED COMMANDS

dtwm	Desktop window manager.
mwm	Motif window manager.
twm	Tab window manager.

openwin *options*

PURPOSE

Starts the X server in an OpenWindows environment, usually called from your **.login** or **.profile** file. **openwin** is a shell script designed to make starting X easier.

OPTIONS

-auth *protocol*	Uses *protocol* instead of the default MIT-MAGIC-COOKIE protocol for access security.
-noauth	Turns off default MIT-MAGIC-COOKIE user-based access security.
-server *server*	Tells **openwin** which program to start as the X server. Defaults to **$OPENWINHOME/bin/Xsun**.
-wm *window_mgr*	Starts *window_mgr* as an alternate window manager instead of the default **olwm**. If you have a **.xinitrc** file in your home directory, this option is likely to be ignored.

RELATED COMMANDS

olwm	Open Look window manager.
startx	Starts X server.
xauth	Creates and modifies X authorization file.

Graphic Commands

shelltool *options*
shelltool *options program args*

PURPOSE

Provides a shell terminal window, much like **cmdtool**, allowing you to enter UNIX commands. You can run multiple **shelltool** windows on your display and copy and paste between them. Inside the window, **shelltool** runs your UNIX shell, which is specified in the SHELL environment variable. Or, you can specify a program and arguments on the command line.

OPTIONS

program args	Runs *program* with arguments instead of your default shell.
-background *red green blue*	Sets background color to *red green blue* values.
-background *color*	Uses *color* for window background.
-bg *color*	Uses *color* for window background.
-C	Captures system console messages and displays in window.
-display *host:disp_num*	Connects to *disp_num* numbered X server (almost always 0) on given *host*.
-fg *color*	Uses *color* for window foreground.
-fn *fontname*	Uses given font.
-font *fontname*	Uses given font.
-foreground_color *red green blue*	Sets foreground color to *red green blue* values.
-foreground *color*	Uses *color* for window foreground.
-geometry *WidthxHeight +x+y*	Sets window size and position.
-geometry *WidthxHeight*	Sets window size.
-geometry *+x+y*	Sets position of window's upper-left corner.

284

Continued

-height *rows*	Sets height of base window, in rows.
-l *command*	Passes *command* to the shell.
-position *x y*	Sets location of upper-left corner of window, in pixels.
-reverse	Reverses foreground and background colors.
-rv	Reverses foreground and background colors.
-size *width height*	Sets base window size, in pixels to *width* x *height*.
-Wb *red green blue*	Sets background color to *red green blue* values.
-Wf *red green blue*	Sets foreground color to *red green blue* values.
-WG *WidthxHeight+x+y*	Sets window size and position.
-WG *WidthxHeight*	Sets window size.
-WG *+x+y*	Sets position of window's upper-left corner.
-Wh *rows*	Sets height of base window, in *rows*.
-Wi	Starts window as an icon.
-width *columns*	Sets width of base window, in *columns*.
-Wp *x y*	Sets location of upper-left corner of window, in pixels.
-Wr *host:disp_num*	Connects to *disp_num* numbered X server (almost always 0) on given *host*.
-Ws *width height*	Sets base window size, in pixels to *width* x *height*.
-Wt *fontname*	Uses given font.
-Ww *columns*	Sets width of base window, in columns.

Graphic Commands

RELATED COMMANDS

cmdtool	Open Look terminal.
dtterm	Common Desktop Environment terminal.
xterm	X terminal.

startx *client_options -- server_options*

PURPOSE

Shell script that starts the X server. **startx** is useful for environments where you do not have a graphical login (usually provided by **xdm**).

OPTIONS

The client options may be either a program to launch in place of the commands in the **.xinitrc** file or options to the default **xterm** program (if no **.xinitrc** file exists in your home directory).

The server options may either be a program to use in place of **X**—the X server—along with options for that program, or options to **X**. See the entry on **X** for the server options.

RELATED COMMANDS

openwin	Starts X server in OpenWindows.
xdm	X display manager.
xinit	Starts X server.

tapetool *options*

PURPOSE

Presents a friendly interface over the **tar** command to allow you to make backups and restore data from tape.

OPTIONS

-background *red green blue*	Sets background color to *red green blue* values.
-background *color*	Uses *color* for window background.
-bg *color*	Uses *color* for window background.
-display *host:disp_num*	Connects to *disp_num* numbered X server (almost always 0) on given *host*.
-fg *color*	Uses *color* for window foreground.
-fn *fontname*	Uses given font.
-font *fontname*	Uses given font.
-foreground_color *red green blue*	Sets foreground color to *red green blue* values.
-foreground *color*	Uses *color* for window foreground.
-geometry *WidthxHeight+x+y*	Sets window size and position.
-geometry *WidthxHeight*	Sets window size.
-geometry *+x+y*	Sets position of window's upper-left corner.
-height *rows*	Sets height of base window, in *rows*.
-position *x y*	Sets location of upper-left corner of window, in pixels.

Graphic
Commands

Continued

-reverse	Reverses foreground and background colors.
-rv	Reverses foreground and background colors.
-size *width height*	Sets base window size, in pixels to *width* x *height*.
-Wb *red green blue*	Sets background color to *red green blue* values.
-Wf *red green blue*	Sets foreground color to *red green blue* values.
-WG *WidthxHeight+x+y*	Sets window size and position.
-WG *WidthxHeight*	Sets window size.
-WG *+x+y*	Sets position of window's upper-left corner.
-Wh *rows*	Sets height of base window, in rows.
-Wi	Starts window as an icon.
-width *columns*	Sets width of base window, in *columns*.
-Wp *x y*	Sets location of upper-left corner of window, in pixels.
-Wr *host:disp_num*	Connects to *disp_num* numbered X server (almost always 0) on given *host*.
-Ws *width height*	Sets base window size, in pixels to *width* x *height*.
-Wt *fontname*	Uses given font.
-Ww *columns*	Sets width of base window, in *columns*.

RELATED COMMAND

tar   Tape archiver.

textedit *options filename*

PURPOSE

Open Look text editor with mouse support.

OPTIONS

-auto_indent	Indents new lines to match line above.
-background *red green blue*	Sets background color to *red green blue* values.
-background *color*	Uses *color* for window background.
-bg *color*	Uses *color* for window background.
-display *host:disp_num*	Connects to *disp_num* numbered X server (almost always 0) on given *host*.
-Ei on	Indents new lines to match line above.
-Ei off	Does not indent new lines to match line above.
-En lines	Sets number of lines in window to *lines*.
-Eo on	Allows you to overwrite an existing file.
-Eo off	Presents an error if you try to over-write an existing file.
-Er on	Prevents you from changing a file; the default is off.
-Er off	Allows you to change files; the default.
-fg *color*	Uses *color* for window foreground.
-fn *fontname*	Uses given font.
-font *fontname*	Uses given font.
-foreground_color *red green blue*	Sets foreground color to *red green blue* values.

Graphic
Commands

289

Continued

-foreground *color*	Uses *color* for window foreground.
-geometry *WidthxHeight+x+y*	Sets window size and position.
-geometry *WidthxHeight*	Sets window size.
-geometry *+x+y*	Sets position of window's upper-left corner.
-height *rows*	Sets height of base window, in rows.
-number_of_lines *lines*	Sets number of lines in window to *lines*.
-okay_to_overwrite	Allows you to overwrite an existing file.
-position *x y*	Sets location of upper-left corner of window, in pixels.
-read_only	Prevents you from changing a file.
-reverse	Reverses foreground and background colors.
-rv	Reverses foreground and background colors.
-size *width height*	Sets base window size, in pixels to *width* x *height*.
-Wb *red green blue*	Sets background color to *red green blue* values.
-Wf *red green blue*	Sets foreground color to *red green blue* values.
-WG *WidthxHeight+x+y*	Sets window size and position.
-WG *WidthxHeight*	Sets window size.
-WG *+x+y*	Sets position of window's upper-left corner.
-Wh *rows*	Sets height of base window, in *rows*.
-Wi	Starts window as an icon.
-width *columns*	Sets width of base window, in *columns*.
-Wp *x y*	Sets location of upper-left corner of window, in pixels.

Continued

-Wr *host:disp_num*	Connects to *disp_num* numbered X server (almost always 0) on given *host*.
-Ws *width height*	Sets base window size, in pixels to *width* x *height*.
-Wt *fontname*	Uses given font.
-Ww *columns*	Sets width of base window, in *columns*.

RELATED COMMANDS

dtpad	Common Desktop Environment text editor.
xedit	Text editor.

Graphic
Commands

toolwait *options application args*

PURPOSE

Starts an X application, then waits for the application to start up and create windows. The *application* and any necessary arguments for the *application* appear at the end of the **toolwait** command.

EXAMPLES

```
toolwait xclock -digital
```

(Starts the **xclock** and passes the **-digital** option to **xclock**.)

```
toolwait -timeout 5 xclock -digital
```

(Starts the **xclock** and passes the **-digital** option to **xclock**, waiting a maximum of 5 seconds for **xclock** to start up.)

OPTION

-display *host:disp_num*   Connects to *disp_num* numbered X server (almost always 0) on given *host*.

twm *options*

PURPOSE

Provides a window manager which controls the size and location of all windows on the screen. Window managers also create the titlebars, many of which are very distinctive.

OPTIONS

-display *host:disp_num*	Connects to *disp_num* numbered X server (almost always 0) on given *host*.
-f *initfile*	Uses *initfile* instead of **.twmrc** in your home directory to configure **twm**.
-s	Manage only windows on the default screen. (Few systems have more than one screen, anyway.)
-v	Prints verbose error messages.

RELATED COMMANDS

dtwm	Common Desktop Environment window manager.
mwm	Motif window manager.
olwm	Open Look window manager.

Graphic
Commands

X *options*

PURPOSE

X is the actual X server program, normally started by **open-win**, **startx**, **xdm**, or **xinit**. **X** controls the monitor screen, keyboard, and mouse. Sometimes the **X** program has an extended name, such as **Xsun** on Sun Solaris systems.

OPTIONS

Some special X servers accept extra options. The options listed here are used by all X servers:

-a *acceleration*	Sets mouse acceleration ratio; defaults to 2.
-audit *level*	Sets audit trail level; defaults to 1. Level 2 logs more information about client applications that connect to the X server. Level 0 disables auditing.
-bs	Disables backing store.
-c	Turns off key click sounds.
c *volume*	Sets key click volume to a value from 0 to 100.
-co *filename*	Uses *filename* for the database of color names.
-core	Server dumps a core file on errors.
-dpi *resolution*	Sets screen resolution in dots per inch. Used when the X server cannot figure this out on its own.
-f *volume*	Sets bell volume to a value from 0 to 100.
-fc *cursor_font*	Uses *cursor_font* as font for cursor shapes, defaults to *cursor*.
-fn *font*	Uses *font* for the default font.
-fp *path1,path2, ...*	Sets list of directories searched for fonts to a comma-delimited list of directories.
-help	Prints a summary of the command-line options.

Continued

-l	Ignores everything after the -l.
-logo	Uses X logo in screen saver.
-nologo	Doesn't use X logo in screen saver.
-p *minutes*	Sets screen saver pattern cycle time to given number of *minutes*.
-pn	Tells server to continue running if a number of socket connections fail, but it gets at least one successfully set up.
-r	Turns off keyboard auto-repeat.
r	Turns on keyboard auto-repeat.
-s *minutes*	Sets screen saver timeout to given number of *minutes*.
-su	Disables save under support for all windows.
-t *number*	Sets mouse acceleration threshold in pixels.
-terminate	Terminates server instead of resetting.
-to *seconds*	Sets connection timeout to *seconds*, defaults to 60.
-tst	Disables all testing extensions including XTEST, XTestExtension1, and XTrap.
-v	Tells screen saver to leave video on.
v	Tells screen saver to turn video off.

RELATED COMMANDS

openwin	Starts X server in OpenWindows.
startx	Starts X server.
xdm	X display manager.
xinit	Starts X server.
xset	Sets X server values.

Graphic Commands

xauth *options command arguments*
xauth *command arguments*

PURPOSE

Creates and modifies a file that controls who can access an X server. **Xauth** has a finer grain of control than **xhost**, which allows any user on a given host to access your display.

XAUTH COMMANDS

COMMAND	MEANING
add *display protocol hexkey*	Adds an entry for the given display; a period (.) is shorthand for a protocol of MIT-MAGIC-COOKIE-1.
extract *filename display...*	Extracts entries for *display* and writes to *filename*; - means stdout.
nextract *filename display...*	Extracts entries for *display* and writes to *filename* using numeric format; - means stdout.
list *display...*	Lists all entries for a given *display*.
nlist *display...*	Lists all entries for a given *display* using numeric output.
merge *filename...*	Merges entries from *filename*; - means stdin.
nmerge *filename...*	Merges entries from *filename* using numeric format; - means stdin.
remove *display...*	Removes all entries for *display*.
source *filename*	Treats filename as a script of **xauth** commands.
info	Prints info on authority file.
exit	Exits and saves authority file.
quit	Exits and doesn't save authority file.
help	Lists all **xauth** commands.

Continued

help *string*	Lists all **xauth** commands starting with *string*.
?	Prints short help message.

EXAMPLES

```
$ xauth add `hostname`/unix:0 . 6666
```

(Adds an X authority entry for unix:0, a common default display name, using the **hostname** command to get the current hostname. The period tells **xauth** to use the MIT-MAGIC-COOKIE-1 protocol, the default protocol. The number 6666 is a random number made up for the occasion.)

```
$ xauth add eric:0 . 6666
```

(Adds an X authority entry for the display name of eric:0, the first X server on machine *eric*. Again, the default protocol and the random number 6666 are used.)

```
$ xauth list
DISPLAY NAME  PROTOCOL NAME          DISPLAY KEY
============  =============          ===========
unix:0        MIT-MAGIC-COOKIE-1     6666
eric:0        MIT-MAGIC-COOKIE-1     6666
```

(Prints a list of all the displays in the **.Xauthority** file.)

```
$ xauth extract - $DISPLAY | \
   rsh eric xauth merge -
```

(Extracts all X authority entries for the current display and passes them on over the network to another program, merging these entries in with the authority file on the target machine, eric. This is a very common use of **xauth**, passing the information needed to log on from one display to another.)

Continued

OPTIONS

-b	Breaks any file locks on the authorization file.
-f *authfile*	Tells **xauth** to use *authfile* as the authorization file. The default is the file named in the XAUTHORITY environment variable or a file named **.Xauthority** in your home directory.
-i	Ignores file locks on the authorization file.
-q	Runs in quiet mode and doesn't print out messages.
-v	Runs in verbose mode and prints out lots of messages to explain what is going on.

RELATED COMMANDS

xdm	X Display Manager.
xhost	Controls access to X server.

xbiff *options*

PURPOSE

Announces new email messages.

OPTIONS

-bd *color*	Uses *color* for window border.
-bg *color*	Uses *color* for window background.
-bw *num_pixels*	Sets border to *num_pixels* wide.
-display *host:disp_num*	Connects to *disp_num* numbered X server (almost always 0) on given *host*.
-file *filename*	Uses *filename* instead of default mailbox file, **/usr/spool/mail/** *username*.
-fg *color*	Uses *color* for window foreground.
-geometry *WidthxHeight+x+y*	Sets window size and position.
-geometry *WidthxHeight*	Sets window size.
-geometry *+x+y*	Sets position of window's upper-left corner.
-help	Prints a summary of the command-line options.
-rv	Reverses foreground and background colors.
-shape	Uses a nonrectangular window.
-update *secs*	Checks for incoming email every *secs* seconds.
-volume *percentage*	Sets volume of bell from 0 to 100.

RELATED COMMANDS

dtmail	Common Desktop Environment email program.
mailtool	Open Look email program.

Graphic Commands

xcalc *options*

PURPOSE

Performs calculations.

OPTIONS

-background *color*	Uses *color* for window background.
-bd *color*	Uses *color* for window border.
-bg *color*	Uses *color* for window background.
-bordercolor *color*	Uses *color* for window border.
-borderwidth *num_pixels*	Sets border to *num_pixels* wide.
-bw *num_pixels*	Sets border to *num_pixels* wide.
-display *host:disp_num*	Connects to *disp_num* numbered X server (almost always 0) on given *host*.
-fg *color*	Uses *color* for window foreground.
-fn *fontname*	Uses given font.
-font *fontname*	Uses given font.
-foreground *color*	Uses *color* for window foreground.
-geometry *WidthxHeight+x+y*	Sets window size and position.
-geometry *WidthxHeight*	Sets window size.
-geometry *+x+y*	Sets position of window's upper-left corner.
-iconic	Starts window as an icon.
-reverse	Reverses foreground and background colors.
-rpn	Uses Reverse Polish Notation.

Continued

-rv   Reverses foreground and back-
                                  ground colors.

-stipple   Draws background using a stipple
                                  of the foreground and background
                                  colors, which makes **xcalc** look bet-
                                  ter on monochrome systems.

RELATED COMMAND

dtcalc   Common Desktop Environment calculator utility.

xclipboard *options*

PURPOSE

Displays the contents of the clipboard and allows you to select that text for pasting into applications.

OPTIONS

-background *color*	Uses *color* for window background.
-bd *color*	Uses *color* for window border.
-bg *color*	Uses *color* for window background.
-bordercolor *color*	Uses *color* for window border.
-borderwidth *num_pixels*	Sets border to *num_pixels* wide.
-bw *num_pixels*	Sets border to *num_pixels* wide.
-display *host:disp_num*	Connects to *disp_num* numbered X server (almost always 0) on given *host*.
-fg *color*	Uses *color* for window foreground.
-fn *fontname*	Uses given font.
-font *fontname*	Uses given font.
-foreground *color*	Uses *color* for window foreground.
-geometry *WidthxHeight+x+y*	Sets window size and position.
-geometry *WidthxHeight*	Sets window size.
-geometry *+x+y*	Sets position of window's upper-left corner.
-iconic	Starts window as an icon.
-nw	Doesn't wrap long lines of text; this is the default.
-reverse	Reverses foreground and background colors.
-rv	Reverses foreground and background colors.
-w	Wraps long lines of text.

Continued

RELATED COMMANDS

dtpad	Common Desktop Environment text editor.
textedit	Open Look text editor.
xedit	X text editor.

Graphic
Commands

xclock *options*

PURPOSE

Displays the time in a window.

EXAMPLES

```
xclock -digital
```

(Displays a digital clock.)

```
xclock -analog -padding 50 -update 1
```

(Displays an analog clock face with 50 pixels of empty space around the clock in all directions, updating every second with a second hand.)

OPTIONS

-analog	Displays an analog clock (with hands).
-background *color*	Uses *color* for window background.
-bd *color*	Uses *color* for window border.
-bg *color*	Uses *color* for window background.
-bordercolor *color*	Uses *color* for window border.
-borderwidth *num_pixels*	Sets border to *num_pixels* wide.
-bw *num_pixels*	Sets border to *num_pixels* wide.
-chime	Chimes once on the half hour and twice on the hour.
-d	Displays a 24-hour digital clock.
-digital	Displays a 24-hour digital clock.
-display *host:disp_num*	Connects to *disp_num* numbered X server (almost always 0) on given *host*.

Continued

-fg *color*	Uses *color* for window foreground.
-fn *fontname*	Uses given font.
-font *fontname*	Uses given font.
-foreground *color*	Uses *color* for window foreground.
-geometry *WidthxHeight+x+y*	Sets window size and position.
-geometry *WidthxHeight*	Sets window size.
-geometry *+x+y*	Sets position of window's upper-left corner.
-hands *color*	Sets the hands to display using the given *color*.
-h *color*	Sets the hands to display using the given *color*.
-highlight *color*	Sets the color for the edges of the clock hands.
-help	Prints a summary of the command-line options.
-hl *color*	Sets the color for the edges of the clock hands.
-iconic	Starts window as an icon.
-padding *pixels*	Sets number of pixels of blank space between the border and the clock.
-reverse	Reverses foreground and background colors.
-rv	Reverses foreground and background colors.
-update *seconds*	Controls update interval. If less than 30 seconds, **xclock** will display a second hand. In that case, it is best to update each second.

RELATED COMMANDS

clock	Open Look clock.
oclock	Rounded clock.

xcmap *options*

PURPOSE

Displays the contents of the default colormap. This is useful for helping with color problems.

OPTIONS

-display *host:disp_num*	Connects to *disp_num* numbered X server (almost always 0) on given *host*.
-geometry *WidthxHeight+x+y*	Sets window size and position.
-geometry *WidthxHeight*	Sets window size.
-geometry *+x+y*	Sets position of window's upper-left corner.

xconsole *options*

PURPOSE

Displays system console messages in a window.

OPTIONS

-background *color*	Uses *color* for window background.
-bd *color*	Uses *color* for window border.
-bg *color*	Uses *color* for window background.
-bordercolor *color*	Uses *color* for window border.
-borderwidth *num_pixels*	Sets border to *num_pixels* wide.
-bw *num_pixels*	Sets border to *num_pixels* wide.
-daemon	Runs in the background.
-display *host:disp_num*	Connects to *disp_num* numbered X server (almost always 0) on given *host*.
-exitOnFail	Tells **xconsole** to exit if it cannot redirect the console output.
-fn *fontname*	Uses given font.
-font *fontname*	Uses given font.
-foreground *color*	Uses *color* for window foreground.
-geometry *WidthxHeight+x+y*	Sets window size and position.
-geometry *WidthxHeight*	Sets window size.
-geometry +*x+y*	Sets position of window's upper-left corner.
-iconic	Starts window as an icon.
-notify	If iconified, adds a "*" to the icon name to let you know a system message has arrived; the default.

Graphic Commands

Continued

-nonotify	Doesn't change icon name to notify of new messages.
-reverse	Reverses foreground and background colors.
-rv	Reverses foreground and background colors.
-verbose	Displays an informative message in the text buffer.

RELATED COMMAND

xterm	Shell window.

xditview *options*

PURPOSE

Displays **ditroff** output files from the device-independent suite of formatting programs called **ditroff**.

OPTIONS

-backingStore *backing_store*	Sets to *Always* or *WhenMapped* to improve performance when redisplaying pages; leave at *NotUseful* if performance is OK.
-background *color*	Uses *color* for window background.
-bd *color*	Uses *color* for window border.
-bg *color*	Uses *color* for window background.
-bordercolor *color*	Uses *color* for window border.
-borderwidth *num_pixels*	Sets border to *num_pixels* wide.
-bw *num_pixels*	Sets border to *num_pixels* wide.
-display *host:disp_num*	Connects to *disp_num* numbered X server (almost always 0) on given *host*.
-fg *color*	Uses *color* for window foreground.
-fn *fontname*	Uses given font.
-font *fontname*	Uses given font.
-foreground_color *red green blue*	Sets foreground color to *red green blue* values.
-foreground *color*	Uses *color* for window foreground.
-geometry *WidthxHeight+x+y*	Sets window size and position.
-geometry *WidthxHeight*	Sets window size.
-geometry *+x+y*	Sets position of window's upper-left corner.
-iconic	Starts window as an icon.
-noPolyText	If text is displayed improperly, this may correct the situation.

Graphic Commands

xditview

Continued

-page *page_number*	Starts with given page.
-resolution *screen_resolution*	Sets screen resolution used when choosing fonts.
-reverse	Reverses foreground and background colors.
-rv	Reverses foreground and background colors.

xdm *options*

PURPOSE

Manages X displays. **xdm** presents a graphical login screen and starts your X session. If you don't have a graphical login screen, then chances are you use **openwin**, **startx**, or **xinit** to start your X session instead of **xdm**.

Normally, **xdm** starts at machine boot time from an entry in **/etc/inittab**, so you will rarely start it from a command line.

OPTIONS

-config *config_file*	Uses *config_file* as the configuration file rather than the default, which is typically **/var/X11/xdm/xdm-config** or **/usr/lib/X11/xdm/xdm-config**.
-debug *debug_level*	Any value above 0 causes **xdm** to run synchronously and print lots of debugging information.
-error *log_file*	Errors get logged to the given *log_file*.
-nodaemon	Stops **xdm** from running in the background as a daemon process.
-resources *res_file*	Names a resource file that customizes the login widget.
-server *server_entry*	Lists the X servers that **xdm** should manage. An entry for the local machine appears like the following: `:0 local /usr/X11/bin/X :0`
-session *session_program*	Names the program to run as a session when the user logs in.
-udpPort *port_number*	Sets the UDP network port for **xdm** to monitor.

(side tab) **Graphic Commands**

Continued

RELATED COMMANDS

openwin	Starts OpenWindows X server.
startx	Starts X server.
X	X server.
xinit	Initializes X server.

xdpr *options*

xdpr *filename options*

PURPOSE

Acts as a front-end to **xwd**, **xpr** and **lp** or **lpr**. **xwd** captures a screen image, **xpr** prepares the image to print and **lp** or **lpr** prints the image. **Xdpr** combines all this into one handy command. If you pass an **xwd**-captured filename to **xdpr**, it prints that file rather than capturing a screen image.

EXAMPLE

```
xdpr -device ps -Pmyhp
```

(Captures a screen image, formats the image for a PostScript printer, and sends the results to the printer named *myhp*.)

OPTIONS

-device *devtype*
: Names the output device type: *la100* (Digital LA100), *ljet* (HP LaserJet), *ln03* (Digital LN03), *pjet* (HP PaintJet in color), *pjetxl* (HP PaintJet XL color), *pp* (IBM PP3812), or *ps* (generic PostScript).

-display *host:disp_num*
: Connects to *disp_num* numbered X server (almost always 0) on given *host*.

-help
: Prints a summary of the command-line options.

-P*printer*
: Names the printer to use for printing. Note there is no space after the **-P**.

Any other options get passed on to **xwd**, **xpr**, **lp** or **lpr**, as appropriate.

Graphic Commands

Continued

RELATED COMMANDS

lp	Prints files.
lpr	Prints files.
xpr	Prints X screen image.
xwd	Captures X screen image.

xdpyinfo *option*

PURPOSE

Prints information about your graphics display, much of which is confusing.

EXAMPLES

```
xdpyinfo
```

(This prints information on your default X server, normally the screen in front of you.)

```
xdpyinfo -display yonsen:0
```

(This prints information on X server yonsen:0, the first—often only—X server running on a machine named *yonsen*.)

OPTION

-display *host:disp_num*   Connects to *disp_num* numbered X server (almost always 0) on given *host*.

RELATED COMMANDS

X	X server.
xrdb	Loads X resource files.
xwininfo	Prints information on windows.

Graphic
Commands

xdvi *options filename*

PURPOSE

Previews DVI files, which are created by TeX.

OPTIONS

+	Displays last page.
+*page_number*	Displays page numbered *page_number*.
-expert	Works in expert mode; doesn't display interface buttons.
-hush	Avoids displaying warning messages.
-hushchars	Avoids displaying warnings about characters not in the current font.
-thorough	Ensures that overstrike characters get properly displayed on color screens.
-version	Prints version number and exits.

RELATED COMMAND

ghostview	Views PostScript Documents.

xedit *options filename*

PURPOSE

Edits text files in a window.

EXAMPLE

```
xedit sigs.txt
```

(Edits file **sigs.txt**.)

OPTIONS

-background *color*	Uses *color* for window background.
-bd *color*	Uses *color* for window border.
-bg *color*	Uses *color* for window background.
-bordercolor *color*	Uses *color* for window border.
-borderwidth *num_pixels*	Sets border to *num_pixels* wide.
-bw *num_pixels*	Sets border to *num_pixels* wide.
-display *host:disp_num*	Connects to *disp_num* numbered X server (almost always 0) on given *host*.
-fg *color*	Uses *color* for window foreground.
-fn *fontname*	Uses given font.
-font *fontname*	Uses given font.
-foreground *color*	Uses *color* for window foreground.
-geometry *WidthxHeight+x+y*	Sets window size and position.
-geometry *WidthxHeight*	Sets window size.
-geometry *+x+y*	Sets position of window's upper-left corner.

Continued

-iconic	Starts window as an icon.
-reverse	Reverses foreground and background colors.
-rv	Reverses foreground and background colors.

RELATED COMMANDS

dtpad	Desktop Text Editor.
textedit	Open Look Text Editor.

xfd *options -fn fontname*

PURPOSE

Displays the characters in a font. **Xfd** is better for showing all of a font, while **xfontsel** is better for choosing a font.

EXAMPLE

```
xfd -fn "-*-courier-medium-r-normal—*-240-*-*-m-*-*"
```

(Displays a courier font.)

OPTIONS

-bc *color*	Uses *color* for boxes with the **-box** option.
-background *color*	Uses *color* for window background.
-bd *color*	Uses *color* for window border.
-bg *color*	Uses *color* for window background.
-bordercolor *color*	Uses *color* for window border.
-borderwidth *num_pixels*	Sets border to *num_pixels* wide.
-box	Shows a box around the actual extents of each character in the font.
-bw *num_pixels*	Sets border to *num_pixels* wide.
-center	Centers each character in its grid.
-columns *numcols*	Sets the number of columns in the grid display.
-display *host:disp_num*	Connects to *disp_num* numbered X server (almost always 0) on given *host*.

319

Continued

-fg *color*	Uses *color* for window foreground.
-fn *fontname*	Uses given font.
-font *fontname*	Uses given font.
-foreground_color *red green blue*	Sets foreground color to *red green blue* values.
-foreground *color*	Uses *color* for window foreground.
-geometry *WidthxHeight+x+y*	Sets window size and position.
-geometry *WidthxHeight*	Sets window size.
-geometry *+x+y*	Sets position of window's upper-left corner.
-iconic	Starts window as an icon.
-reverse	Reverses foreground and background colors.
-rows *numrows*	Sets the number of rows in the grid display.
-rv	Reverses foreground and background colors.
-start *number*	Starts with the character at the given position in the font. Defaults to 0.

RELATED COMMAND

xfontsel   Selects fonts.

xfontsel *options*

PURPOSE

Displays fonts that match a pattern. You can use this to select a desired font style and size.

EXAMPLES

```
xfontsel -sample "Help me choose a font"
```

(Starts **xfontsel** and uses given text to show current font.)

```
xfontsel -pattern "*adobe*"
```

(Selects only *adobe* fonts. Note that since the pattern has asterisks, you need to enclose the pattern in double quotes.)

OPTIONS

-background *color*	Uses *color* for window background.
-bd *color*	Uses *color* for window border.
-bg *color*	Uses *color* for window background.
-bordercolor *color*	Uses *color* for window border.
-borderwidth *num_pixels*	Sets border to *num_pixels* wide.
-bw *num_pixels*	Sets border to *num_pixels* wide.
-display *host:disp_num*	Connects to *disp_num* numbered X server (almost always 0) on given *host*.
-fg *color*	Uses *color* for window foreground.
-fn *fontname*	Uses given font.
-font *fontname*	Uses given font.
-foreground *color*	Uses *color* for window foreground.
-geometry *WidthxHeight+x+y*	Sets window size and position.

321

Continued

-geometry *WidthxHeight*	Sets window size.
-geometry +*x*+*y*	Sets position of window's upper-left corner.
-iconic	Starts window as an icon.
-noscaled	Doesn't display scaled fonts.
-pattern *partial_fontname*	Displays only fonts whose names match *partial_fontname*. Enclose this pattern in double quotes.
-print	Prints selected font name to screen at exit.
-reverse	Reverses foreground and background colors.
-rv	Reverses foreground and background colors.
-sample *sample_text*	Uses *sample_text* rather than alphabet.

RELATED COMMAND

xfd	Displays font.

xfs *options*

PURPOSE

Launches the X font server (previously known as **fs**—without the *x*), which can provide fonts to the X server. It normally adds the ability to scale fonts to a requested size.

OPTIONS

-config *configuration_file*   Sets the configuration file.
-port *tcp_port*   Sets the TCP port number on which the
                                    font server will listen for connections.

RELATED COMMANDS

fsinfo   Gets information on font server.
fslsfonts   Lists fonts provided by a font server.

xhost *options*

PURPOSE

Controls which machines—hosts—can access your X server. Once it is enabled, any user on that machine can connect to your X server. This creates a potential security risk, as a user could track all the keystrokes you enter (including passwords).

EXAMPLE

```
xhost +eric
```

(Allows any user on machine *eric* to connect to your X server.)

OPTIONS

+hostname	Allows any user on host *hostname* to connect to your display.
-hostname	Disallows any user on host *hostname* to connect to your display.
+	Allows any user on any machine to connect to your display.
-	Disallow any extra machines access beyond the list that X starts up with (usually just your machine).

RELATED COMMAND

xauth	Creates authorization file.

xinit *client_options -- server_options*

PURPOSE

Initializes X server. Normally, **xinit** is run from a script such as **startx**. By default, the *client_options* are stored in a file named **.xinitrc** in your home directory and the server options in a file named **.xserverrc**. In most cases, you don't need any *server_options*.

EXAMPLES

```
$ xinit
```

(Starts X server program X and uses **.xinitrc** in your home directory to name the applications to start. If there is no **.xinitrc** file, it starts **xterm**.)

```
$ xinit -- /usr/bin/X11/X -bpp 16
```

(Starts X server with 16 bits-per-plane rather than the default 8 bits of color.)

```
$ xinit -- /usr/bin/X11/X -auth $HOME/.Xauthority
```

(Starts X server using the authorization file **$HOME/ .Xauthority** in your home directory. Usually, **xauth** would create this file for use by X.)

OPTIONS

The client options may be either a program to launch in place of the commands in the **.xinitrc** file or options to the default **xterm** program (if no **.xinitrc** file exists in your home directory).

Graphic Commands

325

Continued

The server options may be either a program to use in place of **X**—the X server—along with options for that program, or options to **X**. See entry on **X** for the server options.

RELATED COMMANDS

startx	Starts X server.
X	X server.
xauth	Creates authorization file to control access to X server.
xdm	X display manager.

xkill *options*

PURPOSE

Kills a window and usually the program that created the window. This is useful for stopping runaway programs.

OPTIONS

-all	Kills all top-level windows.
-button *number*	Determines which mouse button (normally 1 to 3) is used to select the window. Useful for killing popup windows. Defaults to left-most mouse button, 1.
-display *host:disp_num*	Connects to *disp_num* numbered X server (almost always 0) on given *host*.
-frame	Kills framing window rather than window inside a window-manager frame.
-id *ID*	Names the window *ID* to kill. If you omit this, **xkill** asks you to select a window with the mouse.

Graphic Commands

RELATED COMMAND

xwininfo	Prints information on windows.

xload *options*

PURPOSE

Displays system load average.

EXAMPLES

```
xload -highlight maroon -jumpscroll 1
```

(Starts **xload** with maroon-colored scale lines and smooth scrolling.)

```
xload -fg red -bg lightgrey
```

(Starts **xload** with a graph line color of red and a background color of light grey.)

OPTIONS

-background *color*	Uses *color* for window background.
-bd *color*	Uses *color* for window border.
-bg *color*	Uses *color* for window background.
-bordercolor *color*	Uses *color* for window border.
-borderwidth *num_pixels*	Sets border to *num_pixels* wide.
-bw *num_pixels*	Sets border to *num_pixels* wide.
-display *host:disp_num*	Connects to *disp_num* numbered X server (almost always 0) on given *host*.
-fg *color*	Uses *color* for window foreground.
-fn *fontname*	Uses given font.
-font *fontname*	Uses given font.

Continued

-foreground *color*	Uses *color* for window foreground.
-geometry *WidthxHeight+x+y*	Sets window size and position.
-geometry *WidthxHeight*	Sets window size.
-geometry *+x+y*	Sets position of window's upper-left corner.
-hl *color*	Uses *color* for scale lines.
-highlight *color*	Uses *color* for scale lines.
-iconic	Starts window as an icon.
-jumpscroll *pixels*	Specifies number of pixels to shift graph to left when it reaches the end of the window.
-jumpscroll	Uses smooth scrolling.
-label *string*	*String* appears above graph as a label. Default label is system host name.
-lights	Uses keyboard LEDs instead of a window to display load.
-nolabel	Doesn't display a label.
-reverse	Reverses foreground and background colors.
-rv	Reverses foreground and background colors.
-scale *number*	Sets minimum number of tickmarks in graph to *number*.
-update *seconds*	Sets interval in *seconds* between updates to be displayed. Defaults to 10.

Graphic Commands

xlock *options*

PURPOSE

Locks display until you enter your password. The screen is
blanked with a display based on the mode selected.

EXAMPLES

```
xlock -mode bouboule
```

(Locks screen with moving dots display.)

```
xlock -mode world
```

(Locks screen and displays spinning globes.)

OPTIONS

-batchcount *num*	Controls number of *things* based on the mode. For example, in **ant** mode, *num* controls the number of ants.
-bg *color*	Uses *color* for window background.
-cycles *num*	Sets number of cycles until a time-out.
-delay *usecs*	Sets speed for mode drawing in microseconds.
-display *host:disp_num*	Connects to *disp_num* numbered X server (almost always 0) on given *host*.
-fg *color*	Uses *color* for window foreground.
-font *fontname*	Uses given font.

Continued

-lockdelay *seconds*	Sets number of seconds before you need to enter a password. Good for stopping **xlock** before it kicks in.
-mode *mode*	Selects mode to blank screen: **ant, bat, blank, blot, bouboule, bounce, braid, bug, clock, demon, eyes, flag, flame, forest, galaxy, geometry, grav, helix, hop, hyper, image, kaleid, laser, life, life1d, life3d, lissie, marquee, maze, mountain, nose, petal, puzzle, pyro, qix, random, rock, rotor, shape, slip, sphere, spiral, spline, swarm, swirl, triangle, wator, world,** or **worm**.

Graphic Commands

xlogo *options*

PURPOSE

Displays X Window System logo in a window.

OPTIONS

-background *color*	Uses *color* for window background.
-bd *color*	Uses *color* for window border.
-bg *color*	Uses *color* for window background.
-bordercolor *color*	Uses *color* for window border.
-borderwidth *num_pixels*	Sets border to *num_pixels* wide.
-bw *num_pixels*	Sets border to *num_pixels* wide.
-display *host:disp_num*	Connects to *disp_num* numbered X server (almost always 0) on given *host*.
-fg *color*	Uses *color* for window foreground.
-fn *fontname*	Uses given font.
-font *fontname*	Uses given font.
-foreground *color*	Uses *color* for window foreground.
-geometry *WidthxHeight+x+y*	Sets window size and position.
-geometry *WidthxHeight*	Sets window size.
-geometry *+x+y*	Sets position of window's upper-left corner.
-iconic	Starts window as an icon.
-reverse	Reverses foreground and background colors.
-rv	Reverses foreground and background colors.
-shape	Creates a window that is shaped (i.e., X-shaped) rather than rectangular.

xlsfonts *options*

PURPOSE

Lists fonts available to the X server.

EXAMPLES

```
xlsfonts | grep courier
```

(Lists all fonts and pipes output to **grep**, which searches for the text string *courier*.)

```
xlsfonts -lll | more
```

(Lists all fonts, producing copious output including character metrics, and pipes results to **more**.)

OPTIONS

-1	Prints output using only one column; this is the same as **-n 1**.
-C	Prints output in multiple columns; this is the same as **-n 0**.
-display *host:disp_num*	Connects to *disp_num* numbered X server (almost always 0) on given *host*.
-fn *pattern*	Lists fonts that match the *pattern*. * and ? wildcards are allowed. No pattern is the same as *.
-l	Lists some attributes of fonts as well as names.
-ll	Lists font properties in addition to output from **-l** option.
-lll	Prints all of **-ll** output as well as character metrics.

Graphic
Commands

Continued

-m	Prints minimum and maximum bounds of each font.
-n *columns*	Sets number of columns to *columns*.
-o	Gets information on fonts by an alternate means; this is useful if normal listing fails.
-u	Doesn't sort output.
-w *width*	Sets total width of output to *width* characters.

RELATED COMMAND

fslsfonts	List fonts provided by font server.

xmag *options*

PURPOSE

Captures a small screen image and enlarges the data so you can see individual pixels.

OPTIONS

-background *color*	Uses *color* for window background.
-bd *color*	Uses *color* for window border.
-bg *color*	Uses *color* for window background.
-bordercolor *color*	Uses *color* for window border.
-borderwidth *num_pixels*	Sets border to *num_pixels* wide.
-bw *num_pixels*	Sets border to *num_pixels* wide.
-display *host:disp_num*	Connects to *disp_num* numbered X server (almost always 0) on given *host*.
-fg *color*	Uses *color* for window foreground.
-fn *fontname*	Uses given font.
-font *fontname*	Uses given font.
-foreground *color*	Uses *color* for window foreground.
-geometry *WidthxHeight+x+y*	Sets window size and position.
-geometry *WidthxHeight*	Sets window size.
-geometry *+x+y*	Sets position of window's upper-left corner.
-iconic	Starts window as an icon.
-mag *factor*	Magnifies by the given *factor*, which defaults to 5.
-reverse	Reverses foreground and background colors.

Graphic
Commands

Continued

-rv	Reverses foreground and background colors.
-source *WidthxHeight+x+y*	Sets source area size and position.
- source *WidthxHeight*	Sets source area size.
- source *+x+y*	Sets source area upper-left corner. If you don't use a **-source** option, **xmag** asks you to select an area to magnify using the mouse.

xman *options*

PURPOSE

Displays online manuals.

EXAMPLES

```
xman &
```

(Starts **xman** in background.)

```
xman -bothshown
```

(Show both manual entries and the list of available entries.)

```
xman -notopbox
```

(Skips small control window and displays manual entry right away.)

OPTIONS

-background *red green blue*	Sets background color to *red green blue* values.
-background *color*	Uses *color* for window background.
-bd *color*	Uses *color* for window border.
-bg *color*	Uses *color* for window background.
-bordercolor *color*	Uses *color* for window border.
-borderwidth *num_pixels*	Sets border to *num_pixels* wide.
-bothshown	show both manual entries and list of available entries
-bw *num_pixels*	Sets border to *num_pixels* wide.
-display *host:disp_num*	Connects to *disp_num* numbered X server (almost always 0) on given *host*.

Graphic
Commands

Continued

-fg *color*	Uses *color* for window foreground.
-fn *fontname*	Uses given font.
-font *fontname*	Uses given font.
-foreground *color*	Uses *color* for window foreground.
-geometry *WidthxHeight+x+y*	Sets window size and position.
-geometry *WidthxHeight*	Sets window size.
-geometry *+x+y*	Sets position of window's upper-left corner.
-iconic	Starts window as an icon.
-notopbox	Doesn't display small control panel window.
-pagesize *WidthxHeight+x+y*	Displays manual pages in window at given size and location.
-reverse	Reverses foreground and background colors.
-rv	Reverses foreground and background colors.

RELATED COMMAND

man	Prints online manual.

xpr *options*
xpr *options filename*

PURPOSE

Formats an image captured by **xwd** and prepares the image for printing. If you pass a filename, **xpr** formats that file. Otherwise, **xpr** expects data from standard input. The output is sent to standard output unless you specify the **-output** option.

EXAMPLE

```
xpr -device ps capture1.xwd | lp
```

(Formats a previously captured image in file **capture1.xwd** for a PostScript printer and pipes the results to the **lp** command.)

OPTIONS

-append *filename*	Appends output to *filename*.
-compact	Compresses windows with lots of white pixels using run-length encoding.
-cutoff *level*	Sets cutoff level where colors get mapped to black or white to *level* percentage of full brightness.
-density *dpi*	Sets dot-per-inch density for HP printers.
-device *devtype*	Names the output device type: **la100** (Digital LA100), **ljet** (HP LaserJet), **ln03** (Digital LN03), **pjet** (HP PaintJet in color), **pjetxl** (HP PaintJet XL color), **pp** (IBM PP3812), or **ps** (generic PostScript).
-gamma *correction*	Changes intensity of colors for PaintJet XL printers to a *correction* value between 0.00 and 3.00, set according to the printer's manual.
-gray 2	Uses a 2x2 grayscale conversion.
-gray 3	Uses a 3x3 grayscale conversion.

Continued

-gray 4	Uses a 4x4 grayscale conversion.
-header *text*	Uses *text* as a header printed above the image.
-height *inches*	Sets maximum height of output.
-landscape	Sets landscape output.
-left *inches*	Sets left margin.
-output *filename*	Sends output to *filename* rather than to standard output.
-noff	With **-append**, appends image to same page as previous image.
-noposition	Bypasses header, trailer, and positioning for HP LaserJet, PaintJet, and PaintJet XL printers.
-plane *number*	Uses only the given bitplane of the color image.
-portrait	Sets portrait output.
-psfig	Doesn't translate PostScript output to center of page.
-render *algorithm*	Renders image using named *algorithm* from HP PaintJet XL manual.
-rv	Reverses foreground and background colors in output.
-scale *scale*	Sets scaling factor for output.
-slide	Allows HP PaintJet and PaintJet XL printers to create overhead transparencies.
-split *num_pages*	Splits image into a number of pages.
-top *inches*	Sets top margin.
-trailer *text*	Uses *text* as a footer printed below the image.
-width *inches*	Sets maximum width of output.

RELATED COMMANDS

lp	Prints files.
lpr	Prints files.
xdpr	Captures and prints X screen image.
xwd	Captures X screen image.

xprop *options*

PURPOSE

Returns window property information for a given window. You can either specify the window as a command-line option or select the window with the mouse.

X uses window properties to store data about windows, such as requests to the window manager, data exchange, and other information. The root window has interesting properties.

OPTIONS

-display *host:disp_num*	Connects to *disp_num* numbered X server (almost always 0) on given *host*.
-font *font*	Prints properties of given *font*, rather than of a window.
-frame	Selects window-manager frame, rather than window inside frame.
-grammar	Prints detailed information on command-line options.
-help	Prints a summary of the command-line options.
-id *ID*	Prints information for given window *ID*.
-len *length*	Prints at most *length* bytes of any property.
-name *name*	Prints information for window with given *name*.
-notype	Doesn't print the types of properties.
-remove *prop_name*	Removes named property from window.
-root	Prints information for root window (screen background).

Graphic
Commands

Continued

-spy   Keeps checking for property change
                                  events and prints them out as they
                                  occur.

RELATED COMMANDS

xwininfo   Prints window information.
xrdb   Loads resource files.

xrdb *options*
xrdb *options filename*

PURPOSE

Maintains a database of X resource values. With X, you can either use resource files or load the files with **xrdb** into a resource database. Many newer systems, like the Common Desktop Enviroment, make extensive use of **xrdb** and resource databases. If you change a resource in a file such as **.Xdefaults** and it seems to have no effect, you probably need to look into **xrdb**.

For most usage, **xrdb** loads or saves data in a property on the root window called RESOURCE_MANAGER. (If this property exists, resource settings in the **.Xdefaults** file will be ignored by most X applications.) If you pass a *filename* on the command line, **xrdb** will load that file.

EXAMPLES

```
xrdb -query > res1.txt
```

(Reads value of resources in RESOURCE_MANAGER property and writes out data to file **res1.txt**.)

```
xrdb -edit .Xdefaults
```

(Reads value of resources in RESOURCE_MANAGER property and writes out data to file **.Xdefaults**, but preserves anything else already in file **.Xdefaults**.)

```
xrdb -load .Xdefaults
```

(Loads in resources from file **.Xdefaults** into RESOURCE_ MANAGER property on the root window.)

Graphic Commands

Continued

OPTIONS

-all	Sets resources into both RESOURCE_MANAGER and SCREEN_RESOURCES on every screen.
-backup *suffix*	Appends *suffix* to filename used with **-edit** to create a backup file of the original contents.
-cpp *filename*	Uses *filename* in place of **cpp**, the C preprocessor.
-display *host: disp_num*	Connects to *disp_num* numbered X server (almost always 0) on given *host*.
-edit *filename*	Places all resources in the property into the given file, but preserving the rest of the file. This allows you to keep your comments in the file.
-global	Works with RESOURCE_MANAGER property (the default).
-help	Prints a summary of the command-line options.
-load	Loads data from standard input into property, replacing all old values.
-merge	Loads input into property and merges differences.
-n	Prints changes to standard output, but doesn't actually make the changes.
-nocpp	Doesn't preprocess files with **cpp**.
-query	Reads resource values from property.
-quiet	Doesn't print warning messages.
-remove	Removes properties from X server.
-screen	Works with SCREEN_RESOURCES property on the default screen.
-screens	Works with SCREEN_RESOURCES property on all screens.
-symbols	Prints symbols defined by **cpp**.

RELATED COMMANDS

cpp	C preprocessor.
xprop	Prints window properties.

xrefresh *options*

PURPOSE

Repaints all or part of the screen, with a surprisingly large number of options.

EXAMPLES

```
xrefresh
```

(Repaints the screen.)

```
xrefresh -solid orange
```

(Briefly paints the screen orange, then repaints everything.)

OPTIONS

-black	Turns off all electron guns so screen goes black, then repaints.
-display *host:disp_num*	Connects to *disp_num* numbered X server (almost always 0) on given *host*.
-geometry *WidthxHeight+x+y*	Sets window size and position.
-geometry *WidthxHeight*	Sets window size.
-geometry *+x+y*	Sets position of window's upper-left corner.
-none	Repaints all windows with no funny options; the default.
-root	Fills in screen with root window's background color, then repaints.
-solid *color*	Fills in screen with given *color*, then repaints.
-white	Fills in screen with a white background, then repaints.

Graphic Commands

345

xset *options*

PURPOSE

Controls and queries settings in the X server for things like the screen saver blanking timeouts and keyboard repeat rates.

EXAMPLES

```
xset fp rehash
```

(Reloads list of available fonts. Normally done after adding a new font.)

```
xset led on
```

(Turns on all the keyboard LED lights.)

```
xset s off
```

(Turns off screen saver.)

OPTIONS

b on	Turns on bell.
b off	Turns off bell.
b -	Turns off bell.
b *percent*	Sets bell volume to *percent* of maximum.
b *percent pitch duration*	Sets bell volume to *percent* of maximum, at *pitch* hertz and for *duration* milliseconds. Not all hardware allows this control.
c *percent*	Sets key click volume, if supported, to *percent* of maximum.

Continued

c on	Restores defaults for key click volume.
c off	Turns off key click sounds, if supported by hardware.
c -	Turns off key click sounds, if supported by hardware.
-display *host:disp_num*	Connects to *disp_num* numbered X server (almost always 0) on given *host*.
fp= *path,path,...*	Sets font search path to comma-delimited list of directories.
fp default	Restores default set of font search directories.
fp rehash	Tells X server to reload list of available fonts.
-fp *path,path,...*	Removes comma-delimited list of directories from font search path.
fp- *path,path,...*	Removes comma-delimited list of directories from font search path.
+fp *path,path,...*	Adds comma-delimited list of directories to font search path.
fp+ *path,path,...*	Adds comma-delimited list of directories to font search path.
led -	Turns off all keyboard LED lights.
led on	Turns on all keyboard LED lights.
led off	Turns off all keyboard LED lights.
led *number*	Turns on keyboard LED light *number*, e.g., 3 for the third light.
-led *number*	Turns off keyboard LED light *number*.
m *accelt_mult threshold*	Sets mouse acceleration. *accelt_mult* controls how much faster the mouse should move when accelerating, e.g., two times faster, while *threshold* controls the distance the mouse must move, in pixels, in a short period of time to start accelerating.

Graphic
Commands

Continued

p *pixel color*	Sets colormap ID number *pixel* to given *color*.
r	Turns on key autorepeat (when you hold down a key).
-r	Turns off key autorepeat.
s off	Turns off screen saver.
s on	Turns on screen saver.
s *noblank*	Uses a pattern rather than a blank screen for screen saver.
s *timeout pattern*	Sets screen saver to turn on with *timeout* seconds of inactivity and change its pattern (if there is any) every *pattern* seconds.

xsetroot *options*

PURPOSE

Changes the root window—the screen background—from
the default X cross-hatch pattern to a bitmap pattern or
solid color.

If you use the Common Desktop Environment, you
must set the screen background to "No Background" in the
Style Manager (**dtstyle**) before calling **xsetroot** to change the
screen background, or you will see no effect.

EXAMPLES

```
xsetroot -cursor_name gumby
```

(Sets default cursor to the Gumby shape.)

```
xsetroot -cursor_name gumby -bg green
```

(Sets default cursor to the Gumby shape with a green background color.)

```
xsetroot -solid bisque2
```

(Sets screen background color to **bisque2**, which is easy on
the eyes.)

OPTIONS

-bg *color*	Uses *color* for window background.
-bitmap *filename*	Tiles bitmap in given file for screen background, using current screen foreground and background colors.

Continued

-cursor *cursorfile maskfile*	Sets default cursor to given image and mask. Both files can be created by the bitmap program.
-cursor_name *cursorname*	Sets default cursor to given named cursor, e.g., *gumby*.
-def	Resets all unspecified values to defaults. The screen background gets a black and white cross-hatch mesh and the cursor becomes an X.
-display *host:disp_num*	Connects to *disp_num* numbered X server (almost always 0) on given *host*.
-fg *color*	Uses given foreground *color*; only works with **-bitmap**, **-cursor**, **-cursor_name**, or **-mod**.
-gray	Sets entire background gray.
-grey	Sets entire background gray.
-help	Prints summary of the command-line options.
-mod *x y*	Creates a plaid using numbers *x* and *y* from 1 to 16.
-name *name*	Sets name of root window to *name*.
-rv	Reverses foreground and background colors.
-solid *color*	Fills screen background with given *color*.

RELATED COMMANDS

bitmap	Creates bitmap files.
dtstyle	Sets Common Desktop Environment settings.

xterm *options*

PURPOSE

Provides a shell terminal window that acts much like a VT102 terminal, allowing you to enter UNIX commands. You can run multiple **xterm** windows on your display and copy and paste between them. Inside the window, **xterm** runs your UNIX shell, which is specified in the SHELL environment variable. You can control the fonts used and whether or not to display a scrollbar. **xterm** remains the most-used X application because it allows you to directly enter UNIX commands.

EXAMPLES

```
xterm -sb &
```

(Starts **xterm** with a scrollbar in the background—very useful.)

```
xterm -fn "-*-courier-medium-r-normal—18-*-*-*-m-*-*" &
```

(Starts **xterm** using the given courier font. See **xlsfonts** for a list of fonts.)

OPTIONS

-132	Allows **xterm** to honor the DECCOLM escape sequence that switches between 80 and 132 column mode.
-ah	Always highlights text cursor.
+ah	Only highlights the text cursor when the window has the keyboard focus; the default.
-background *color*	Uses *color* for window background.

Continued

-bd *color*	Uses *color* for window border.
-bg *color*	Uses *color* for window background.
-bordercolor *color*	Uses *color* for window border.
-borderwidth *num_pixels*	Sets border to *num_pixels* wide.
-bw *num_pixels*	Sets border to *num_pixels* wide.
-C	Captures console output. Makes **xterm** similar to **xconsole**.
-cn	Doesn't cut newlines when selecting to the end of a line.
+cn	Cuts newlines when selecting to the end of a line.
-cr *color*	Sets text cursor color.
-display *host:disp_num*	Connects to *disp_num* numbered X server (almost always 0) on given *host*.
-e *program args*	Executes *program* with its arguments *args* instead of the default shell.
-fb *fontname*	Uses *fontname* for bold items.
-fg *color*	Uses *color* for window foreground.
-fn *fontname*	Uses given font.
-foreground *color*	Uses *color* for window foreground.
-geometry *Width*x *Height+x+y*	Sets window size and position.
-geometry *Width*x*Height*	Sets window size.
-geometry *+x+y*	Sets position of window's upper-left corner.
-help	Prints a summary of the command-line options.
-iconic	Starts window as an icon.
-j	Turns on jump scrolling.
+j	Turns off jump scrolling.
-ls	Starts **xterm** as a login shell. Use this if **xterm** doesn't properly read your start-up files, like **.login** for the C shell or **.profile** for the Korn shell.

352

Continued

-mb	Rings a bell when you type near the end of the line. Very annoying.
-reverse	Reverses foreground and background colors.
-rv	Reverses foreground and background colors.
-rw	Allows reverse wraparound. This means the cursor can back up from the start of one row to the end of the previous row.
-s	Allows asynchronous scrolling, which is useful for slow networks.
-sb	Displays a scrollbar to allow you to recall data that scrolls by.
+sb	Doesn't display a scrollbar.
-si	Scrolls window to bottom when new output appears.
+si	Turns off **-si** mode.
-sk	Scrolls window to bottom when you type in text.
+sk	Turns off **-sk** mode.
-sl *number*	Sets the number of lines in the scrolling buffer, defaults to 64.
-t	Starts in Tektronix mode, not VT102 mode.
+t	Starts in VT102 mode, the default.
-title *string*	Sets window title.

RELATED COMMANDS

cmdtool	Open Tool shell window.
dtterm	Common Desktop Environment shell window.
shelltool	Open Tool shell window.
xconsole	Displays console messages.
xlsfonts	Lists available fonts.

xv options filenames

PURPOSE

This wonderful graphics display and screen capture program supports most image file formats. You can display single images or use the "visual schnauzer" to view directories. The right mouse button displays the **xv** controls window, from which most functions are available. **xv** is not available on all systems.

EXAMPLES

```
xv &
```

(Starts image browser in background.)

```
xv lion.gif
```

(Displays image file **lion.gif**.)

```
xv -quit -root -max lion.gif
```

(Displays image file **lion.gif** on the background of the screen—the root window—and expands as necessary to fit the screen. Quits the application once the image is loaded.)

OPTIONS

-cemap	Starts with color editor window, too.
+cemap	Starts without color editor window.
-cmap	Starts with control window, too.
+cmap	Starts without control window.
-display *host:disp_num*	Connects to *disp_num* numbered X server (almost always 0) on given *host*.

Continued

-dir *directory*	Starts visual schnauzer in given *directory*.
-help	Prints a summary of the command-line options.
-iconic	Starts window as an icon.
-imap	Starts with image information window, too.
+imap	Starts without image information window.
-quit	Quits after performing actions requested on command line.
-wait *seconds*	Waits for given time.
-root	Displays images on root window rather than in **xv**'s window.
-vsmap	Starts with visual schnauzer window, too.
+vsmap	Starts without visual schnauzer window.

RELATED COMMANDS

xwd	Captures screen image.
xwud	Displays captured screen image.

Graphic
Commands

xwd *options*

PURPOSE

Captures an image of a window and saves it to a file. Unfortunately, the **xwd** image format tends to be rather obscure and works mostly with tools like **xwud** and **xpr**. The **xv** program can convert this format to other more common image formats, such as GIF or JPEG.

xwd will prompt you to select a window if you have not selected a window by its ID, name, or the root window.

EXAMPLE

```
xwd -name xterm -add 45 -out image1.xwd
```

(Captures the window named *xterm*, adds 45 to every color pixel value to darken the image, and writes the output to the file **image1.xwd**.)

OPTIONS

-add *value*	Adds *value* to every pixel. Can be used to lighten or darken an image. Negative numbers generally lighten; positive numbers darken.
-display *host:disp_num*	Connects to *disp_num* numbered X server (almost always 0) on given *host*.
-frame	Captures window manager frame along with window; used only in interactive mode.
-help	Prints a summary of the command-line options.

Continued

-icmap	Uses the first installed colormap of the screen for colors rather than the colormap for the window.
-id window_id	Captures the window with the given ID.
-name name	Captures the window with the given **name**.
-nobdrs	Doesn't include the window border when capturing image.
-out filename	Stores output in filename rather than sending output to the terminal.
-root	Captures the root window.
-screen	Captures any areas that overlap the window, too.
-xy	Uses XY format for dumping color images, rather than the default Z format.

RELATED COMMANDS

xv	Image viewer.
xwud	Undumps an X window.

Graphic
Commands

xwininfo *options*

PURPOSE

Prints information about a given window. In interactive mode, you can select the window or use a window ID.

EXAMPLES

```
xwininfo -root -children -all
```

(Displays all possible information about the root window, as well as information about all of its children, that is, all windows.)

```
xwininfo -all
```

(Asks you to select a window, then displays all available information.)

OPTIONS

-all	Displays all possible information.
-bits	Prints out the bit flags for the selected window, including the backing-store and save-under hints.
-children	Prints information about the selected window as well as the names and IDs of all children and the parent of the selected window.
-display *host:disp_num*	Connects to *disp_num* numbered X server (almost always 0) on given *host*.
-english	Displays data in inches as well as pixels.
-events	Prints out the event masks for the selected window.

Continued

-frame	Selects the frame rather than the inner window.
-help	Prints a summary of the command-line options.
-id *window_id*	Prints information about the given window.
-int	Prints window IDs as decimal rather than hexadecimal values.
-metric	Displays data in millimeters as well as pixels.
-name *window_name*	Prints information about the window with the given name.
-root	Prints information about the root window (screen background).
-shape	Prints the window's border and shape extents (if not rectangular).
-size	Prints the requested sizes (including maximum and minimum) of the selected window.
-stats	Prints information about the location and color map for the selected window.
-tree	Prints full information about the selected window, its parent, and all of its children. Very useful with the **-root** option.
-wm	Prints the window manager hints for the selected window.

Graphic
Commands

xwud *options*

PURPOSE

Displays an image captured by **xwd**. **xwud** quits when you click a mouse button in the window or when you type **q, Q,** or **Ctrl-C**.

EXAMPLES

```
xwud -in image3.xwd
```

(Loads up image stored in file **image3.xwd**.)

```
xwd -root | xwud
```

(Captures the root window and then displays the image captured.)

OPTIONS

-bg *color*	Uses *color* for window background.
-display *host:disp_num*	Connects to *disp_num* numbered X server (almost always 0) on given *host*.
-fg *color*	Uses *color* for window foreground.
-geometry *WidthxHeight+x+y*	Sets window size and position.
-geometry *WidthxHeight*	Sets window size.
-geometry *+x+y*	Sets position of window's upper-left corner.
-help	Prints a summary of the command-line options.
-in *filename*	Displays image stored in *filename* rather than the default, which assumes the image is passed as standard input.

Continued

-new	Creates a new colormap to display the image.
-noclick	Disables mouse clicks from quitting **xwud**.
-plane *number*	Displays a single bit plane of an image. This can be used with **xpr** for printing a single bit plane.
-raw	Uses the raw color IDs in the default colormap.
-rv	Reverses the foreground and background colors for monochrome images.

RELATED COMMANDS

xdpr	Dumps an X window and prints it.
xpr	Prints an X window dump.
xwd	Dumps an X window.

Graphic Commands

Programming Commands

UNIX is a great programming environment. In this short section, we've listed some of the most commonly used programming commands. These commands won't make you into a programmer, but they should give you an idea of the UNIX conventions regarding programming.

ar *key files*

PURPOSE

Maintains an archive—called a library—of compiled software modules. These library routines are then used when creating UNIX programs.

EXAMPLE

```
ar rv libFOO.a module1.o module2.o
```

(Adds—or replaces if necessary—the modules **module1.o** and **module2.o** in the library file **libFOO.a**.)

OPTIONS

r	Replaces files in archive with new files.
s	Updates symbol table.
t	Prints table of contents (list of files in archive).
v	Works in verbose mode; combined with another option, prints messages.

You must supply one of the **r**, **s**, or **t** options.

RELATED COMMANDS

cc	C compiler.
CC	C++ compiler.

cc *options files*

PURPOSE

This command compiles C language programs (source files, assembler source files, or preprocessed C source files).

 There are literally dozens of options available for this command. Check your system documentation or online manual page for a full set.

EXAMPLE

```
$ cc -o hello hello.o
```

(This creates an executable file named **hello** from an object module named **hello.o**.)

OPTIONS

-c *filename*	Specifies the name of the file to compile to generate an **.o** file.
-g	Generates debugging information.
-l *library*	Link in the given library, e.g., -lX11.
-o *filename*	Specifies the name of the executable file to generate.
-O	Optimizes while compiling.

RELATED COMMAND

CC	C++ compiler.

CC *options files*

PURPOSE

Compiles C++ files and creates executable programs. Note that CC, which compiles C++ code, differs from **cc** (all low-ercase), which compiles C code.

 There are literally dozens of options available for this command. Check your system documentation or online manual page for a full set.

EXAMPLE

```
CC -o myprog myprog.cxx
```

(Compiles the C++ code file **myprog.cxx** and creates an executable program named **myprog**.)

OPTIONS

-c *filename*	Specifies the name of the file to compile to generate an **.o** file.
-g	Generates debugging information.
-l *library*	Link in the given library, e.g., **-lm** for **libm.a**.
-o *filename*	Specifies the name of the executable file to generate.
-O	Optimizes while compiling.

RELATED COMMANDS

ar	Creates software libraries.
cc	C compiler.

ci *options file*
ci *options file1 file2 ...*

PURPOSE

Checks a file or files into the Revision Control System, or RCS. You must have a directory named **RCS** for this command to work.

 There's a lot more to the Revision Control System, or RCS. See the online manual information on rcsintro for a good overview of RCS.

EXAMPLE

```
ci -l fred.cxx
```

(Checks in file **fred.cxx** and then checks out again, locking the file.)

OPTIONS

-l	Checks in file after check in using **co -l**.
-rrev	Assigns revision number *rev* to checked-in file.
-u	Checks in file—unlocked—after check out.

RELATED COMMANDS

co	Checks out files from RCS.
rcs	Manipulates files in RCS.

Programming
Commands

co *options file*

co *options file1 file2 ...*

PURPOSE

Checks a file or files out of the Revision Control System, or RCS. You must have a directory named **RCS** for this command to work.

 NOTE There's a lot more to the Revision Control System, or RCS. See the online manual information on rcsintro for a good overview of RCS.

EXAMPLES

```
co -l fred.cxx
```

(Checks out file **fred.cxx**, locking the file so you can modify it.)

```
co -u fred.cxx
```

(Checks out file **fred.cxx**, but does not lock the file.)

OPTIONS

-l	Checks out file after check in using **co -l**.
-r*rev*	Assigns revision number *rev* to checked-out file.
-u	Checks out file, unlocked.

RELATED COMMANDS

ci	Checks in files to RCS.
rcs	Manipulates files in RCS.

dbx *program*

dbx *program core*

PURPOSE

One of many UNIX debuggers. The most common are **dbx**, **gdb**, and **xdb**. It is likely your system will have only one of these three debuggers. A debugger helps you find bugs in a running program by allowing you to examine the parts of the code as they get executed. To make this happen, you must compile your code with the **-g** option to **cc** or **CC** to provide information crucial to the debugger. Debuggers can usually work in one of two modes: with a running program or in postmortem mode by examining the core file created when the program crashed.

Dbx is common on Sun and Silicon Graphics systems.

EXAMPLES

```
dbx myprog
```

(Starts debugger working with program **myprog**.)

```
dbx myprog core
```

(Starts debugger working with program **myprog** and using core dump file named **core**.)

RELATED COMMAND

xdb   Hewlett-Packard UNIX debugger.

make *options*

PURPOSE

Builds programs the most efficient way, based on file modification dates. If a code file has changed, **make** will rebuild the code file but won't rebuild everything else. To use **make**, you need to create a **Makefile**, much like the following:

```
OBJS=    str.o mytest.o

mytest:        $(OBJS)
         CC -o mytest $(OBJS)

INC=     -I.

str.o:    str.cxx
         CC -c $(INC) str.cxx

mytest.o:       mytest.cxx
         CC -c $(INC) mytest.cxx
```

The rules in the file above describe how to recompile the executable program **mytest** if either of the code files, **str.cxx** or **mytest.cxx**, has changed.

EXAMPLES

```
make -f MyMakefile
```

(Uses the file **MyMakefile** instead of the default **Makefile**.)

```
make str.o
```

Continued

(Builds **str.o** rather than the default target—the first target in the **Makefile**.)

OPTIONS

-f *Makefile*	Names an alternative Makefile.
-n	Works in no-execute mode; **make** just prints out the commands it would execute.
target	Builds given target.

RELATED COMMANDS

ar	Creates software libraries.
cc	C compiler.
CC	C++ compiler.

rcs *options file*
rcs *options file1 file2...*

PURPOSE

Changes attributes of files stored within the Revision Control System, or RCS.

 There's a lot more to the Revision Control System, or RCS. See the online manual information on rcsintro for a good overview of RCS.

OPTIONS

-i	Creates and initializes a new file without any file contents.
-l	Locks file without modifying it. Useful if you've made changes but didn't first check out the file.
-u	Abandons changes to file, unlocking it.

RELATED COMMANDS

ci	Checks in files to RCS.
co	Checks out files from RCS.

xdb *program*
xdb *program core*

PURPOSE

One of many UNIX debuggers. The most common are **dbx**, **gdb**, and **xdb**. It is likely your system will have only one of these three debuggers. A debugger helps you find bugs in a running program by allowing you to examine the parts of the code as they get executed. To make this happen, you must compile your code with the **-g** option to **cc** or **CC** to provide information crucial to the debugger. Debuggers can usually work in one of two modes: with a running program or in postmortem mode by examining the core file created when the program crashed.

Xdb is the default HP-UX debugger on Hewlett-Packard systems. It works best from an **hpterm** window rather than an **xterm** window.

EXAMPLE

```
xdb myprog core
```

(Starts debugger working with program **myprog** and using core dump file named **core**.)

RELATED COMMAND

dbx   UNIX debugger.

6

System-Administration Commands

These system-administration commands are geared primarily toward the system administrator, and some of them are available only for privileged users. However, others—particularly the at command and related commands—can also come in handy for the majority of UNIX system users. If you think you could use any of these commands but are currently barred from doing so, check with your system administrator.

at *option1 time [date] increment*

at *option2 [job-id]*

PURPOSE

The **at** command performs specified commands at given times and dates, as long as the commands require no additional input from you. For instance, you may want to print a series of long documents at midnight so you won't tie up the laser printer for hours when other people may need it. You don't need to interact with the laser printer at midnight (although you should make sure its paper tray is filled before leaving work!), so you can use the **at** command to print at that time.

There are two of sets options available with the **at** commands. One set of options, which we'll call *option1*, relates to setting the targeted time and date. The second set of options, which we'll represent with *option2*, allows changes to jobs already scheduled. After you enter the **at** command, you type in the commands to execute at that time. You type in these commands at the keyboard. When you're finished, press **Ctrl-D**. At the given time, **at** runs your commands. Any output from the commands is sent to you via electronic mail.

Even though the at command is used primarily by system administrators, it can also be used by regular users, but this usage must be set by the system administrator. If you are not authorized to use at, you'll see an error message like the following: at: you are not authorized to run at. Sorry. If you want to use the at command, talk with your system administrator.

Continued

EXAMPLES

```
$ at 11am
ls
Ctrl-D
```

(**at** reads the command to run from standard input. On the line following the command line, you enter commands and end with **Ctrl-D**.)

```
$ at 11am nov 1
$ at 11am nov 1, 1997
$ at 11am sun
$ at now + 2 weeks
$ at [option2] [job-id]
```

 Job-IDs are issued by the system when a job is scheduled.

SCHEDULING OPTIONS

-f *filename*   Executes the commands listed in *filename*. Not available on all systems.

-m   Notifies user when job is completed.

TIME OPTIONS

time   Obviously, the time when the commands should run. Unless you specify otherwise (with am or pm as a suffix), the system assumes military time.

midnight   These options are used in lieu of a specific time. If
noon   you use **now** as an option, you must specify an
now   increment (see below).

System-Administration
Commands

Continued

DATE OPTIONS

date	Format is usually specified as *month day, year*, with year optional.
day	The specific day when the command should run, with the name either spelled out (*Sunday*) or referred to by the first three letters (*Sun*).
today	These options are used in lieu of a specific date.
tomorrow	

ALREADY-SCHEDULED JOBS OPTIONS

-l	Lists current job.
-r	Removes specified job.

INCREMENT OPTION

increment	A numerical value relative to the current time and date. The increment must contain a reference to **minute**, **hour**, **day**, **week**, **month**, or **year**. In the example at the beginning of this command's listing (*at now + 2 weeks*), the job would be performed two weeks from now.

RELATED COMMANDS

atq	Immediately prints jobs scheduled with the **at** command.
atrm	Removes jobs scheduled by **at**.
batch	Runs a series of commands in order in the background.

atq *option user*

PURPOSE

Prints jobs already scheduled with the **at** command. There's
not a lot of control available with the command: You can
print all the jobs, print all the jobs generated by a specific
user, or print the jobs in the order they were generated
through the **at** command.

 **Even though the atq command is used primarily by sys-
tem administrators, it can also be used by regular users,
but this usage must be set by the system administrator.
If you want to use the atq command, talk with your system administrator.**

OPTIONS

-c   Sorts the print queue in the order jobs were generat-
            ed through the **at** command.

-n   Returns the number of jobs in the print queue but
            does not print them.

RELATED COMMANDS

at   Schedules jobs to be performed at a specific time.

atrm   Removes jobs scheduled by **at**.

atrm *option user job-id*

PURPOSE

Removes jobs already scheduled with the **at** command.
Privileged users can remove *all* jobs or the jobs of a specific
user, while other users can remove only those jobs generated by themselves.

OPTIONS

-a   Removes all jobs generated by the current user only.
-i   Removes the job only after the approval of the user
                (**y** or **n**).

RELATED COMMANDS

at   Schedules jobs to be performed at a specific time.
atq   Immediately prints jobs scheduled with the **at** com-
                mand.

batch

PURPOSE

Runs a series of commands one command at a time in the background, avoiding the performance issue of running several commands simultaneously in the background.

EXAMPLE

```
batch
pr -a kevinstuff
lp kevinstuff
Ctrl-D
```

OPTIONS

None.

System-Administration
Commands

chgrp *options groupname filename(s)*

PURPOSE

This changes the ownership of a file or files to a new or existing group, specified by either name (stored in **/etc/group**) or ID number. File owners can use the command to change the ownership of only their own files, while privileged users can use the command to change ownership of any file. This command can also be used to change the IDs for an entire directory and the files within.

EXAMPLE

```
$ chgrp restricted kevin.report
```

(This changes the group for **kevin.report** to **restricted**.)

```
$ chgrp -R restricted /usr/users/kevin/reports
```

(This changes the group for all the files and subdirectories within **/usr/users/kevin/reports** to **restricted**.)

OPTIONS

-h   Changes a symbolic link, not the file referenced by a symbolic link. Not available on all systems.

-R   Recursively changes through subdirectories and files.

group   Either a group name (stored in **/etc/group**) or ID number.

RELATED COMMANDS

chown   Changes file ownership.

chmod   Changes file-access permissions.

newgrp   Changes to a new working group.

cpio -i *options*
cpio -o *options*
cpio -p *options*

PURPOSE

Copies archived files to and from backup storage devices like tape drives. This rather involved command is meant for true system administrators, not for those of us who putz around with system-administration commands as the need arises. Because of this, we suggest that you check your system documentation before using this command. Besides, the **tar** command is much easier to work with.

System-Administration
Commands

crontab *filename*

PURPOSE

The **crontab** command sets up a file containing a list of tasks to be performed regularly, such as data backups and regular correspondence. The **crontab** command creates the file (if none exists) from keyboard entry, or processes a text file generated by a text editor. The **cron** program then runs those commands.

The syntax of this file is very rigid. There are six fields to a file, each separated by a space. The first five fields specify exactly when the command is to be run; the sixth field is the command itself. The first five fields are:

FIELD	MEANING
1	Minutes after the hour (0–59)
2	Hour, in 24-hour format (0–23)
3	Day of the month (1–31)
4	Month (1–12)
5	Day of the week (0–6; the 0 refers to Sunday)

Asterisks (*) specify when commands are to be run in every instance of the value of the field. For instance, an asterisk in the Month field would mean that the command should be run every month. In addition, multiple events can be scheduled within a field; merely separate all instances with commas—with no space between.

EXAMPLES

To run a command every morning at 9:30 a.m., the line in the **crontab**-generated file would look like this:

```
30 9 * * * command
```

Continued

To run a command at 1 p.m. only on the 1st and 15th of the
month, the line in the **crontab**-generated file would look
like this:

```
0 13 1,15 * * command
```

To install the events file in your system, making it operational, use the **crontab** command:

```
$ crontab events_file
```

 Although crontab is a command primarily meant for system administrators, it's useful for any user. BSD or pre-
System V users, however, are out of luck, as those systems allow use of crontab only for system administrators.
If you're using a newer version of UNIX and want to use
this command, check with your system administrator.

OPTIONS

-e   Edits the current **crontab** file or creates a new one.
                Not available on all systems.

-l   Lists the contents of the **crontab** file.

-r   Removes the **crontab** file.

RELATED COMMAND

at   Runs a command at a specified time.

login *options*

PURPOSE

This command logs you on the UNIX system. Without this command, there's not a lot of computing work you can finish.

If you do not supply a username with the **login** command, you'll be prompted for one. In addition, **login** may ask you for a password, if your system is so configured.

OPTIONS

username	Supplies a *username* when you login.
var=value	Changes the *value* of an environment variable.

RELATED COMMAND

logname	Login name.

newgrp *option group*

PURPOSE

Logs you into a new *group* during a current session. If you do not have permission to join a group, the request will be denied.

OPTION

-           Changes to the new group, with new environment associated with the new *group*.

RELATED COMMANDS

chgrp   Changes group.
env   Sets environment.

stty *options modes*

PURPOSE

Displays your terminal configuration and options. If you use **stty** with no options or modes, your current configuration will be returned in basic format; use **stty -a** for a more complete—and cryptic—listing of your current configuration.

As UNIX hardware evolves, the use of the **stty** command becomes less and less common. Unless you're really into hardware and want to start mucking around with modes and settings, we advise you to shy away from the **stty** command, except in one situation: When you dial into a UNIX host and find that the Backspace key does not work. Try the following:

```
$ stty erase backspace
```

Don't type the word 9; instead, press the actual **Backspace** key on your terminal. This should fix the problem.

OPTIONS

-a   Displays current options and their settings.
-g   Displays current settings.

tput *options capname*

PURPOSE

Displays information about your terminal's capabilities, as contained in the **terminfo** database (usually stored in the **/usr/lib/terminfo** directory). While you can use the **tput** command to directly manipulate your terminal—for instance, the command **tput clear** will clear the screen—this capability is used mostly by programmers and certainly not by beginning UNIX users.

OPTIONS

-T*type*	Returns the capabilities of terminal *type*. If no *type* is specified, **tput** uses the current terminal as the default.
init	Returns initialization strings and expands tabs.
longname	Returns the long name of your terminal.

RELATED COMMAND

stty　　Sets terminal modes.

tty *options*

PURPOSE

Returns the operational settings for your terminal. This command is often used in shell scripts to see if the script is being run from a terminal.

OPTIONS

-a   Displays all settings. Not available on all systems.

-s   Displays only codes: 0 (terminal), 1 (not a terminal), or 2 (invalid option).

RELATED COMMAND

stty   Changes terminal settings.

7

Shell Commands and Variables

A shell is a command like every other UNIX command. If you've already browsed through the commands listed in Chapter 5, you'll see that the C shell, the Bourne shell, and the Korn shell were all listed as commands. All three shells do the same thing: They act as interpreters, translating your commands into a form the operating system can understand. When you log in a UNIX system, you automatically launch a shell program; without it, you wouldn't be able to do a whole lot with UNIX.

As noted in Chapter 1, a shell uses a special symbol to show that it's ready and waiting for a command from you. The Bourne and Korn shells typically use the $ symbol, while the C shell uses the % symbol. (If you're logged on the system as a privileged user—also known as the superuser or the root user—you'll have a # as your prompt.)

Most users configure their system with the shell when they log in the system (this is known as setting your *environment variables*, which are contained in a file referenced in your **.profile** file) or perform some special tasks with **shell scripts**. The analog to DOS batch files, shell scripts are exactly what the name implies: They are a script of commands performed by the system on command.

This chapter covers the most important shell variables, followed by some choice shell commands. We do not cover *every* shell variable, nor do we cover *every* shell command. Using variables and shell commands is considered an intermediate to advanced topic; see the Bibliography for a listing of books that will help you on your way toward advanced shell usage.

Bourne and Korn Shell Variables

The Bourne shell has the distinction of being the original shell in UNIX. The newer Korn shell was designed as an improvement of the Bourne shell, incorporating several useful traits from the C shell (such as command history) while retaining the familiar structure of the Bourne shell.

Unless noted, the variables listed below are valid for both the Korn and Bourne shells. The following is not a full list of shell variables, but merely the most useful and popular ones. Check your documentation or a book listed in the Bibliography for more information on shell variables.

VARIABLE	MEANING
CDPATH	Tells the shell where to look for a relative pathname, which allows you to enter shorter command lines. For instance, if you used the following line: **CDPATH=/usr/users/kevin/data** in your **.profile** file, you wouldn't need to refer to the full pathname every time you wanted to refer to that directory. You can list multiple directories as long as they are separated by colons (:).
COLUMNS	Sets the number of columns across your display. The default is 80. (Korn shell.)
EDITOR	Sets the default text editor, usually **emacs** or **vi**. Some commands and other applications call an editor. (Korn shell.)
ENV	Establishes the location of the environment file (usually **.kshrc**). (Korn shell.)
HISTSIZE	Sets the history list size. *History* refers to commands already executed; the list can be referenced on the command line by number. (Korn shell.)
HOME	When you login a system, you're immediately placed in your **HOME** directory. When you use the **cd** command with no parameters, you're automatically placed back into that directory.
IFS	Stands for *Internal Field Separator*. The prompt uses spaces, tabs, and newlines to separate items on a command line. If you were to set the **IFS** to **&**, the prompt would use that symbol to separate items on a command line.

Variable	Meaning
LOGNAME	Stores the current user's login name. (Korn shell.)
MAIL	Designates your mail file, where **mailx** or another mail program automatically sends your incoming mail.
MAILCHECK	Tells the shell how often to check for mail (the default is every 10 minutes), measured in seconds. A setting of **MAILCHECK=3600** checks for mail every hour; a setting of **MAILCHECK=0** checks for mail every time a prompt appears on the screen (not the most efficient use of computing resources).
MAILPATH	Designates multiple mail files.
PATH	Sets the file-search path. If you screw up and mistakenly have the system check for multiple files, you could end up spending a lot of time as the shell searches through a large file system. Since most of your frequently used files are in the same directories, this allows you to tell the system where to look for commands.
PS1	Stands for _Primary Shell_ prompt (the default is $). A line like `PS1="Wake up!"` would establish a prompt of `Wake up!`
PS2	Sets the secondary shell prompt (the default is >). The secondary prompt is used when a command runs over a single line.
SHELL	Sets the subshell, which is used by commands like **vi** or **ed**.
TERM	Stands for _terminal_ type. For instance, a setting of `TERM=VT100` sets the terminal type for VT100, which is a popular terminal type.
TERMINFO	Stands for _terminal information_, stored in the **/usr/lib/terminfo** database. (Korn shell.)
TMOUT	Sets the timeout value, which is the period of inactivity (in seconds) before the system logs a user out. (Korn shell.)
TZ	Stands for _Time zone_, which is referenced by the **date** command. For instance, if you were in the Central Time Zone with daylight savings time, you'd normally use **TZ=CST6CDT**. (Korn shell.)

The time zone format may be different on your version of UNIX. Check your system documentation.)

C Shell Variables

The C shell dates from the 1970s, when it was originated at the University of California as a more advanced shell. This shell is so named because of its resemblance to the C programming language, although it does make for a nice little pun.

The following is not a full list of shell variables, but merely the most useful and popular ones. Check your documentation or a book listed in the Bibliography for more information on shell variables.

Variable	Meaning
cdpath	Tells the shell where to look for a relative pathname, which allows you to enter shorter command lines. For instance, if you used the following line: **CDPATH=/usr/users/kevin/data** in your .cshrc file, you wouldn't need to refer to the full pathname every time you wanted to refer to that directory. You can list multiple directories as long as they are separated by colons (:).
echo	Displays full commands, including substitutions.
history	Sets the history list size. *History* refers to commands already executed; the list can be referenced on the command line by number.
HOME	When you login a system, you're immediately placed in your **HOME** directory. When you use the **cd** command, you're automatically placed back into that directory.
mail	Designates your mail file, where **mailx** or another mail program automatically sends your incoming mail.
notify	Informs you when a job is completed.
PATH	Sets the file-search path. If you screw up and mistakenly have the system check for multiple files, you could end up spending a lot of time as the shell searches through a large file system. Since most of your frequently used files are in the same directories, this allows you to tell the system where to look for commands.

Variable	Meaning
prompt	Sets the prompt, which informs you that the shell is waiting for a command. The default is %.
savehist	Determines the number of commands to be saved in your **.history** file, which received input thanks to the **history** command.
shell	This sets the subshell, which is used by commands like **vi** or **ed**.
TERM	Stands for *term*inal type. For instance, a setting of **TERM=VT100** sets the terminal type for VT100, which is a popular terminal type.
USER	Stores the current user's login name.

Shell Commands and Scripts

When you use a shell, you enter commands at the shell's prompt (usually $ or %). You can enter any of the commands described in this book in Chapters 5 and 6, as well as a number of shell commands. These commands exist only in a particular shell, such as the **alias** command in the C shell (described in the "C Shell Commands" section later in this chapter).

In addition to entering commands at the prompt, you can also write **shell scripts**, which are sets of shell commands stored in an ASCII text file. Shell scripts are an easy way to store commonly used sets of UNIX commands. DOS users call shell scripts **batch files**. In DOS, these files have a **.BAT** extension. In UNIX, though, you are free to name your shell scripts anything you desire (providing you desire a valid UNIX filename, of course).

Shell scripts use both the same commands that you could type in at the shell prompt ($ or %) and some of the complex commands described below. It's usually easier to write a shell script and use it as needed that to reissue the commands whenever you want to do a common task.

You'll find that many of the following commands smack of programming. No, we're not out to make you programmers, but it is useful to know what these commands do, especially if you need to write a short shell script on your own. For more advanced shell scripting, check your documentation or a book listed in the Bibliography.

Empowering a Shell Script to Run

You store shell scripts in ASCII text files. Before you can try out a shell script, you must tell UNIX that your ASCII text file really does contain commands. To do this, you can use the **chmod** command (described in Chapter 5):

```
$ chmod +x my_shell_script
```

You need to enable the execute permission on the shell script's file. In the above example, we used **chmod** to enable the execute permission (**+x**) on the file **my_shell_script**.

Once you do this, you can execute your shell script by typing in the filename. For example:

```
$ my_shell_script
```

Comments

It's always wise to describe what a shell script does, so that when you look it up months from now you know why you originally wrote it. To help describe what is going on, you can include **comments**. A comment in a shell script begins with a # character at the start of the line. Any other text—to the end of the line—is treated as a comment; that is, the shell ignores this text. For example:

```
# This is a comment.
```

Comments apply equally to the Bourne, Korn, and C shells.

Bourne and Korn Shell Commands

When you're writing shell scripts, you often need to control what happens based on certain conditions. For example, you may want to copy the 1997 report to another directory using the **cp** command. But, if the 1997 report is not done yet (that is, if the file does not exist), you may want to take other action, such as notifying the user that the report is missing. You can use the **echo** command to display a message for the user.

However, you don't want to run both the **echo** command (with an error message) and the **cp** command. To control which command gets executed, you can use the **if-then** command.

If-Then

The Bourne and Korn shells allow you to run a command (or set of many commands) only under certain conditions. The problem is that you must format these conditions in a way that the shell understands. Format your **if-then** commands in the following way:

> **if test** *expression*
> **then**
>   *command1*
>   *command2*
>   *command3*
>   ...
> **fi**

Basically, **if-then** uses the built-in **test** command (which we cover below) to determine whether or not to run a set of commands. These commands are placed after **then** and before **fi**. (**Fi** stands for **if** backwards.) You can place any number of commands you need between **then** and **fi**. For example:

```
# Check if 5 is indeed 5.
if test 5 = 5
    then
        echo "5 equals 5"
fi
```

This example tests whether 5 is the same as 5. If so, it echoes (prints out) a statement to that effect.

The Test Command

The **test** command is both a UNIX command and a shell command. **Test** returns a true value if the expression you pass to it is true. Otherwise, **test** returns a false value. The shell **if** command uses **test** to determine whether or not to execute the code between **then** and **fi**.

You can use many options with **test** when writing complex shell scripts. Most of these options delve into areas far too advanced for this beginning book. One option that you'll see a lot in shell script files, though, is the cryptic use of square brackets. You can use square brackets, [ ], as shorthand for the **test** command. For example:

```
if [ 5 = 5 ]
    then
        echo "5 still equals 5"
fi
```

For other **test** options, check your documentation or a book listed in the Bibliography.

If-Then-Else

Sometimes you need to perform a set of commands if the condition in an **if-then** command is *not* met, as well as if the condition is met. In that case, you can use **if-then-else**, which uses the following format:

```
if test expression
   then
     command1
     command2
     command3
     ...
   else
     command1
     command2
     command3
     ...
 fi
```

If the **test** expression is true, then the shell executes the commands between **then** and **else**. Otherwise, the shell executes the commands between **else** and **fi**. For example:

```
if test 4 = 5
   then
      echo "4 equals 5"
   else
      echo "4 does not equal 5"
fi
```

If you run this, you should see that four does not equal five.

For Loops

The **for** command allows you to write a shell script that loops through a set of values, performing the same commands repeatedly. Most commonly, you want to loop through a set of files and perform the same operation on each file. The **for** command repeats a set of commands over a set of values for a given variable. The **for** command uses the following format:

> **for** *variable*
>   **in** *values*

do
> *command1*
> *command2*
> *command3*
> ...

done

It often is important to place the **in** statement on its own line.

All commands between **do** and **done** get executed each time through the loop. Each time through the loop, your *variable* will have one of the values. For example:

```
for filename
    in *.1997
    do
        echo $filename
done
```

The variable **filename** will hold the name of a file ending in *.1997*, such as **jan.1997**, **feb.1997**, and **dec.1997**, each time through the loop.

C Shell Commands

The C shell provides the same basic set of control commands, such as **if-then-else**, as do the Bourne and Korn shells. However, the C shell uses its own syntax, which tends to be confusing at times.

If-Then

Like the Bourne and Korn shells, the C shell provides an **if-then** statement. In the C shell, it has a slightly different format:

> **if** *(expression)* **then**
> > *command1*

```
        command2
        command3
        ...
    endif
```

For example:

```
if (5 == 5) then
      echo "5 does indeed equal 5"
endif
```

Note the use of == (two equal signs) rather than =. In addition, with the C shell, you must place **then** on the same line as **if**.

If-Then-Else

You can also use an **if-then-else** statement:

> **if** *(expression)* **then**
>   *command1*
>   *command2*
>   *command3*
>   ...
> **else**
>   *command1*
>   *command2*
>   *command3*
>   ...
> **endif**

For example:

```
if (4 == 5) then
      echo "4 equals 5"
   else
      echo "4 does not equal 5"
endif
```

This example should print out:

```
does not equal 5
```

Foreach

Instead of a command named **for**, the C shell provides a **foreach** command, but the effect is nearly the same:

> **foreach** *variable (list-of-values)*
>   *command1*
>   *command2*
>   *command3*
>   ...
> **end**

For example:

```
foreach filename (*.1997)
     echo $filename
end
```

This example lists all files that end with *.1997*. Each time through the loop, the variable **filename** holds one of the file-names (ending in *.1997*).

Using Alias to Change Identities

In addition to the commands above, the C shell offers the handy **alias** command:

alias new-name old-command

For example, if you're more experienced with DOS than UNIX, you may be confused by all the options to the UNIX **ls** command. With **alias**, you can define your own command named *dir*, which acts more like the DOS **DIR** command:

```
alias dir      ls -alx
```

This command aliases **dir** for the more complex (and harder to remember) command of **ls -alx**. Thus, when you type in **dir**, the C shell actually executes **ls -alx**; you'll see a long-format directory listing, which is about the closest UNIX equivalent to the DOS **DIR** command.

With **alias**, you're extending the set of commands offered by UNIX. This is very useful, particularly if you're moving to UNIX from another operating system, like DOS or VMS.

8

FTP Commands

One undeniable advantage of being on the Internet is access to widely available free software. While we often dial into remote machines and grab interesting software, this process is not easy for the average computer user. As with almost everything else in the UNIX world, the commands are geared for the expert—in other words, someone who already knows what they are doing.

If you are on the Internet, you can use the **ftp** program to transfer files to and from remote machines. (If you're not sure whether you're on the Internet, check with your system administrator.) **Ftp** stands for *File Transfer Protocol*, and it's rapidly becoming the most popular way to grab files from another networked computer. The **ftp** program is easy to use. To start it, type:

```
$ ftp
ftp>
```

Your shell prompt will be replaced with an **ftp** prompt. At this point you can enter the commands listed in this chapter.

You can establish a direct connection to a machine in tow ways. You can specify the machine's name when you begin an **ftp** session:

```
$ ftp machine_kevin
```

or you can use the **open** command after starting an **ftp** session:

```
ftp> open
(to) machine_kevin
Connected to machine_kevin
```

Anonymous FTP

Normally, when you use the **ftp** command, you must have an account set up on the remote machine. Since it's rather impractical to set up an account for every user in a high-traffic situation, the practice of **anonymous ftp** evolved. This allows you to log on a remote machine as **anonymous**. Your privileges on the machine are extremely limited—you're allowed mainly to upload and download files from a specific directory, and that's about it—but this setup works very well.

To use anonymous ftp, you initiate an **ftp** session in the normal way except that you enter *anonymous* as your name, with your email address (referred to as your *ident*) as your password:

```
ftp> open
(to) machine_kevin
Connected to machine_kevin
Name (machine_kevin): anonymous
220 Guest login ok, send ident as password.
Password: kreichard@mcimail.com
230 Guest login ok, access restrictions apply.
```

From there you use the regular **ftp** commands.

A Listing of FTP Commands

Here's a rundown on the commands to use once you're online. If you're not sure which command to use, don't be afraid to experiment. You can't do a whole lot of damage, and the worst that can happen is you might be booted off the system.

Some of the commands used during an ftp session are standard UNIX commands. We've flagged them down for you, should you want more information.

Command	Purpose
! *command*	Runs a shell.
$ *macros arg(s)*	Runs a *macro*, along with an optional *argument*.
? *command*	Displays help for specified *command*.
account *password*	Sets up a new account, with a new *password*.
append *file1 file2*	Appends the local file *file1* to the remote file *file2*.
ascii	Sets transfer mode to ASCII (text) format. This is the default.
bell	Creates a sound (usually a beep) after a file is transferred.
binary	Sets transfer mode to binary format.
bye	Ends ftp session and ends the **ftp** program.
cd *directory*	Changes the current remote directory to *directory*.
	CD is a standard UNIX command. See Chapter 5, "UNIX Commands, Organized by Group," for more information on this command.
cdup	Changes the current directory to one level up on the directory hierarchy. Same as cd ...
close	Ends ftp session with the remote machine but continues the **ftp** command on the local machine.
debug	Turns debugging on or off. (The default is off.)
delete *filename*	Removes *filename* from remote directory.
dir *directory filename*	Returns the contents of the specified *directory*; resulting information is stored in *filename* as specified.
disconnect	Ends ftp session and **ftp** program.

FTP Commands

COMMAND	PURPOSE
get *file1 file2*	Gets *file1* from the remote machine and stores it under the filename *file2*. If *file2* is not specified, the *file1* name will be retained. This command works the same as the RECV command.
hash	Returns status while transferring numbers by returning feedback for each block transferred.
help *command*	Displays information about specified *command*; displays general help information if no *command* is specified.
lcd *directory*	Changes the current local directory to the specified *directory*. If *directory* is not specified, the current local directory changes to the home directory.
ls *directory filename*	Lists the contents of the directory (if *directory* is specified; otherwise, the contents of the current directory will be listed). If a *filename* is specified, then information about the specified file will be listed. **LS is a standard UNIX command. See Chapter 5, "UNIX Commands, Organized by Group," for more information on this command.**
macdef *macrofile*	Defines a macro, ending with a blank line; the resulting macro is stored in the file *macrofile*.
mdelete *filename(s)*	Deletes *filename(s)* on the remote machine.
mdir *filename(s)*	Returns directory for multiple, specified *filename(s)*.
mget *filename(s)*	Gets the specified multiple *filename(s)* from the remote machine.
mkdir *directory*	Makes a new directory, named *directory*, on the remote machine. **MKDIR is a standard UNIX command. See Chapter 5, "UNIX Commands, Organized by Group," for more informa-**tion on this command.

Command	Purpose
mput *filename(s)*	Puts the specified *filename(s)* on the remote machine.
open *remote_machine*	Opens a connection to the specified remote machine. If no remote machine is specified, the system will prompt you for a machine name.
put *file1 file2*	Puts local file *file1* on the remote machine, under the new filename *file2*. If *file2* is not specified, the file will retain the name *file1*.
	This command works the same as the **SEND** command.
pwd	Returns the current directory on the remote machine. (No, this command has nothing to do with a password. This acronym actually stands for *print working directory*, if you find this easier to remember.)
quit	Terminates connection to remote machine and ends the **ftp** program.
recv *file1 file2*	Retrieves *file1* from remote machine and stores it as *file2* on your computer (if you specify *file2*, that is).
	This command works the same as the **GET** command.
remotehelp *command*	Returns help information about a specific *command* from the remote machine, not from the help files on your computer.
rename *file1 file2*	Renames *file1* on the remote system to the new *file2*.
rmdir *directory*	Removes *directory* from the remote machine.
	RMDIR is a standard UNIX command. See Chapter 5, "UNIX Commands, Organized by Group," for more information on this command.
send *file1 file2*	Puts local file *file1* on the remote machine, under the new filename *file2*. If *file2* is not specified, the file will be retain the name *file1*.
	This command works the same as the **PUT** command.

FTP
Commands

RELATED COMMANDS

9

Window Managers

A *window manager* controls the look and feel of your display if you're running the X Window System, OSF/Motif, or the Common Desktop Environment. It controls how and where windows are placed on your screen, what they look like, and how data is input. In addition, a window manager also controls things like icons and mouse actions.

The most popular window manager in the UNIX/X world is the Motif Window Manager, **mwm**. A commercial offering of the Open Group (formerly from a separate cor Open Software Foundation), **mwm** is sold on its own, and it also serves as the basis of the **dtwm** window manager, which is the core of the Common Desktop Environment (CDE). Other popular window managers include the Open Look Window Manager (**olwm**), the Tab Window Manager (**twm**), and the **fvwm** window manager that is usually part of Linux. These window managers are free.

The level of user tools differs between **mwm** and **dtwm**. Generally, **dtwm** offers a fuller environment, complete with session and style managers, as well as a full set of user tools (in Chapter 5, anything beginning with *dt* under "Graphical Commands" is part of the **dtwm** command set). A Front Panel centralizes these functions.

Most of the time, a window manager is configured to perform basic tasks in a way that won't attract your attention—you won't be driven to change the defaults or the way the window manager acts. However, if you do want to change the look and feel of your window manager, there's an easy way to make changes. We're not going to spend time detailing how the **mwm** and **dtwm** window managers work, but we will briefly discuss how to configure them.

Command-Line Options

These command-line options can be invoked when the **dtwm** and **mwm** window managers are launched.

OPTION	PURPOSE
-display *display*	Specifies a display to use upon startup.
-xrm *resourcestring*	Specifies a resource string.
-multiscreen	Manages all screens; this is the default with **dtwm**, and it is usually the default with **mwm**.
-name *name*	Retrieves resources from *name*, as in *name*resource*.
-screens *name* [*name* [...]]	Specifies resource names for screens managed by **dtwm** and **mwm**.

Resources

Resources control the appearance of the window manager and how it interacts with you and application. These resources are stored in a resource file. Typically, this resource file for the **dtwm** window manager can be found at **/usr/dt/app-defaults/$LANG/Dtwm** or **$HOME/Dtwm**, while resource information for **mwm** can be found at **/usr/lib/X11/app-defaults/Mwm** or **$HOME/Mwm**. (There are other locations for these files, as explained in the **mwm** and **dtwm** documentation.)

What will you find in these files? Generally, information regarding files containing bitmaps, fonts, and window-manager–specific resources like menus and behavior specifications. There are resource names and resource classes, with names in lowercase and classes in uppercase, and the resource name having precedence over the resource class. There are the following types of resources associated with **mwm** and **dtwm**:

- Component-appearance resources, which control menus, frames, icons, and other interface elements. The available resources are listed in Table 9.1.

- General appearance and behavior resources, which control how the window manager interact with other applications and applying to all screens and workspaces. The available resources are listed in Table 9.2.

- Screen-specific appearance and behavior resources, which are resources applied on a per-screen basis. These are listed in Table 9.3.

- Client-specific resources, which are set for a particular client window or class of client windows. These are listed in Table 9.4.

- Workspace-specific resources, which apply to a specific workspace. These are listed in Table 9.5, but they apply only to the **dtwm** window manager.

These names are combined with the name of the window manager; for instance, to set the background resource, you'd use *Dtwm*background*. Similarly, to set the keyboard focus to a particular client window, you'd use *Dtwm*keyboard-FocusPolicy*.

Table 9.1 Component-Appearance
Resources for Dtwm and Mwm

NAME	CLASS	VALUE TYPE	SETS...
background	Background	*color*	background color; any valid X value will do.
backgroundPixmap	BackgroundPixmap	*image_file*	the image of the window decoration when the window is not active.
bottomShadow Color	Foreground	*color*	right bevels of the window-manager decoration; any valid X value will do.
bottomShadow Pixmap	Foreground	*image_file*	right bevels of the window-manager decoration.
fontList	FontList	*font_name*	font used in the window-manager decoration; the default is fixed.
foreground	Foreground	*color*	foreground color; any X color will do
saveUnder	SaveUnder	T/F	whether save-unders are used; this is when the contents of windows obscured by the windows are saved. The default is F (false).
topShadowColor	Background	*color*	the top shadow color, on the upper and left bevels.

Name	Class	Value Type	Sets...
topShadowPixmap	TopShadowPixmap	*image_file*	the top shadow pixmap on the upper and left bevels.
activeBackground	Background	*color*	the background color of the decoration when the window is active.
activeBackground Pixmap	BackgroundPixmap	*image_file*	the background pixmap of the decoration when the window is active.
activeBottom ShadowColor	Foreground	*color*	the bottom shadow color of the decoration when the window is active.
activeBottom ShadowPixmap	BottomShadow Pixmap	*image_file*	the bottom shadow pixmap of the decoration when the window is active.
activeForeground	Foreground	*color*	the foreground color of the decoration when the window is active.
activeTopShadow Color	Background	*color*	the top shadow color of the decoration when the window is active.
activeTopShadow Pixmap	TopShadow Pixmap	*image_file*	the top shadow pixmap of the decoration when the window is active.

Window
Managers

Table 9.2 General Appearance and Behavior
Resources for dtwm and mwm

NAME	CLASS	VALUE TYPE	SETS...
autoKeyFocus	AutoKeyFocus	T/F	focus when a window with focus is withdrawn from window management or is iconified; the default (T) sets the focus on the previous window with focus.
autoRaiseDelay	AutoRaiseDelay	*millisec*	the time that the window manager will wait before raising a window after it gets keyboard focus.
bitmapDirectory	BitmapDirectory	*directory*	directory containing bitmaps. The default is **/usr/include/X11/ bitmaps**.
clientAutoPlace	ClientAutoPlace	T/F	the position of a window that has no default position; the default is to position a window with the top left corners of the frames offset horizontally and vertically.
colormapFocus Policy	ColormapFocus Policy	**value**	the colormap focus policy, one of *explicit* (colormap selection action is done on a client window to set the colormap focus to that window), *pointer* (client window containing the pointer has the colormap focus), or *keyboard* (client window with the keyboard input has the colormap focus).

Name	Class	Value Type	Sets...
configFile	ConfigFile	*filename*	the location for the default configuration file; the default for **dtwm** is **$HOME/dtwmrc**, and the default for **mwm** is **.mwmrc**.
deiconifyKeyFocus	DeiconifyKeyFocus	T/F	whether a deiconified window has focus.
doubleClickTime	DoubleClickTime	*num*	the time between clicks in a double-click, in milliseconds.
enableWarp	enableWarp	T/F	the pointer to the center of the selected window during keyboard-controlled resize and move operations if True.
enforceKeyFocus	EnforceKeyFocus	T/F	key focus.
frameStyle	FrameStyle	*value*	the frame style: *slab* (the client area appears to be at the same height as the top of the window frame) or *recessed* (where the client area appears lower than the top of the window frame. (**dtwm** only.)
iconAutoPlace	IconAutoPlace	T/F	the placement of an icon, as determined by the iconPlacement setting.
iconClick	IconClick	T/F	whether a system menu is left posted when an icon is clicked.

Window Managers

417

NAME	CLASS	VALUE TYPE	SETS...
interactive Placement	Interactive Placement	T/F	the initial placement of a window; T lets the user set the placement, while F uses the application configuration defaults.
keyboardFocus Policy	KeyboardFocus Policy	*value*	keyboard focus: *explicit* (where the user explicitly chooses a window) or *pointer* (where the pointer determines the window with focus).
lowerOnIconify	LowerOnIconify	T/F	if an icon should be placed on the bottom of the screen (T) or in the same location as the window (F).
marqueeSelect Granularity	MarqueeSelect Granularity	*pixels*	how often changes in the marquee selection are reported to the window manager.
moveThreshold	MoveThreshold	*pixels*	maximum number of pixels before a move operation is initiated; the default is 4.
multiScreen	MultiScreen	T/F	if the window manager should manager all screens (T) or only a single screen (F).
passButtons	PassButtons	T/F	if button-press events are passed to clients after performing a window-manager function.

NAME	CLASS	VALUE TYPE	SETS...
passSelectButton	PassSelectButton	T/F	if select button-press events are passed to clients after performing a window- manager function.
positionIsFrame	PositionIsFrame	T/F	how window-position information is interpreted: as the position of the window-manager frame (T) or the client area (F).
positionOnScreen	PositionOnScreen	T/F	whether windows should be initially be placed so they are not clipped by the edge of the screen.
quitTimeout	QuitTimeout	*value*	the time (in milliseconds) that the window manager will wait for a client to update the WM_COMMAND property after being warned.
raiseKeyFocus	RaiseKeyFocus	T/F	whether a window raised by the f.normalize_and_ raise function should receive the input focus.
refreshByClearing	RefreshByClearing	T/F	the mechanism for refreshing a screen: T performs XClearArea, while F creates a new window and destroys the old one.
rootButtonClick	RootButtonClick	T/F	whether a click on the root window posts the root menu in "sticky" mode. (**dtwm** only.)

Window
Managers

NAME	CLASS	VALUE TYPE	SETS...
screens	Screens	*value*	the resource names to use for managed windows.
showFeedback	ShowFeedback	value	whether feedback windows or confirmation dialog windows are displayed.
startupKeyFocus	StartupKeyFocus	T/F	whether a window gets keyboard focus when the window is mapped.
useFrontPanels	useFrontPanel	T/F	the display of the front panel. (dtwm only.)
wMenuButton Click	WMenuButtonClick	T/F	whether a click of the mouse when the pointer is over the window menu button posts and leaves posted the window menu.
wMenuButton Click2	WMenuButton Click2	T/F	a double-click on the window menu button does an f.kill function.

Table 9.3 Screen-Specific Appearance and Behavior Resources for Dtwm; These Are General Settings for Mwm

NAME	CLASS	VALUE TYPE	SETS...
buttonBindings	ButtonBindings	*value*	button bindings.
cleanText	CleanText	T/F	the display of window-manager text in client title and feedback windows: T draws with a clear (no stipple) background, while F draws directly on the existing background.

NAME	CLASS	VALUE TYPE	SETS...
fadeNormalIcon	FadeNormalIcon	T/F	whether an icon is grayed after the window has been normalized.
feedbackGeometry	FeedbackGeometry	*value*	the position of the move and resize feedback window.
frameBorderWidth	FrameBorderWidth	*num*	the size of the border width, in pixels.
iconBoxGeometry	IconBoxGeometry	*value*	the initial position and size of the icon box
iconBoxName	IconBoxName	*value*	icon-box resource names.
iconBoxSBDisplay Policy	IconBoxSBDisplay Policy	*string*	the scrollbar policy: *all*, *vertical*, or *horizontal*.
iconBoxTitle	IconBoxTitle	*string*	the title of the icon box.
iconDecoration	IconDecoration	*value*	the general icon decoration.
iconImage Maximum	IconImage Maximum	*w***x***h*	the maximum size of the icon image.
iconImage Minimum	IconImage Minimum	*w***x***h*	the minimum size of the icon image
iconPlacement	IconPlacement	—	the icon placement scheme.
iconPlacement Margin	IconPlacement Margin	*num*	the distance between the edge of the screen (in pixels) and the icons placed along the edge of the screen.
keyBindings	KeyBindings	*string*	key bindings.
limitResize	LimitResize	T/F	a user can exceed the maximum window size.
maximum MaximumSize	Maximum MaximumSize	*w***x***h*	the maximum size of a window, in pixels.

421

NAME	CLASS	VALUE TYPE	SETS...
moveOpaque	MoveOpaque	T/F	whether the actual window or an ghosted representation of a window is moved.
resizeBorderWidth	ResizeBorderWidth	*num*	the border of a frame border, in pixels.
resizeCursors	ResizeCursors	T/F	whether resize cursors are always displayed.
transientDecoration	TransientDecoration	*string*	amount of decoration on transient windows
transientFunctions	TransientFunctions	*string*	which window-management functions are available to transient windows.
useIconBox	UseIconBox	T/F	whether icons should be placed in an icon box.
workspaceCount	WorkspaceCount	*num*	initial number of workspaces that the window manager reates when starting. (**dtwm** only.)

Table 9.4 Client-Specific Resources for Dtwm and Mwm

NAME	CLASS	VALUE TYPE	SETS...
clientDecoration	ClientDecoration	*string*	the amount of window frame decoration.
clientFunctions	ClientFunctions	*string*	which **dtwm** functions are appropriate for the client.
focusAutoRaise	FocusAutoRaise	T/F	whether clients are raised when they have the focus.

NAME	CLASS	VALUE TYPE	SETS...
iconImage	IconImage	*pathname*	icon image for a client.
iconImage Background	Background	*color*	the color of an icon background.
iconImageBottom Foreground	ShadowColor bottom shadow.	*color*	the color of an icon
iconImageBottom ShadowPixmap	Pixmap	*pixmap*	the pixmap of the bottom shadow of an icon.
iconImage Foreground	Foreground	*color*	the color foreground of an icon image.
iconImageTop ShadowColor	Background	*color*	the top shadow color of the icon image.
iconImageTop ShadowPixmap	TopShadowPixmap	*color*	the top shadow pixmap of the icon image.
matteBackground	Background	*color*	background color of the matte.
matteBottom ShadowColor	Foreground	*color*	the bottom shadow color of the matte.
matteBottom ShadowPixmap	BottomShadow Pixmap	*pixmap*	the bottom shadow pixmap of the matte.
matteForeground	Foreground	*color*	the foreground color of the matte.
matteTop ShadowColor	Background	*color*	the top shadow color of the matte.
matteTop ShadowPixmap	TopShadowPixmap	*color*	the top shadow pixmap of the matte.
matteWidth	MatteWidth	*value*	the width of the optional matte.
maximumClientSize	MaximumClientSize	*w**x**h*	either a size specification or a direction that indicates how a client window is to be maximized.

Window
Managers

NAME	CLASS	VALUE TYPE	SETS...
useClientIcon	UseClientIcon	T/F	whether a client-supplied icon should take precedence over a user-supplied icon.
usePPosition	UsePPosition	*string*	whether the position in WM_NOR-MAL_ HINTS property is to honored.
windowMenu	WindowMenu	*string*	the name of the menu pane.

Table 9.5 Workspace-Specific Resources for Dtwm

NAME	CLASS	VALUE TYPE	SETS...
title	Title	*string*	the workspace name.
colorSetId	ColorSetId	*num*	the color set for a backdrop.
image	Image	*string*	the image to use as the backdrop.
imageBackground	ImageBackground	*pixel*	the color to use in the background of a backdrop.
imageForeground	ImageForeground	*pixel*	the color to use in the foreground of a backdrop.

Bibliography

If you've picked this book out from the shelves of your friendly community bookstore, you've already discovered that there are *a lot* of UNIX books on the market. Most of them are on the advanced level and are geared toward programmers and system administrators. Other titles are geared for such a small and specialized audience (most UNIX users don't need guides on **sendmail** and **perl**, for instance). If you take away those titles and focus on the ones meant for the larger end-user community, you're left with a much smaller list. Of these, we recommend the following.

General Titles

Teach Yourself UNIX, third edition. Kevin Reichard and Eric F. Johnson, MIS:Press, 1996. This introduction to the UNIX operating system is designed as a companion to this book. Most of the commands listed in this work are more fully explained in *Teach Yourself UNIX*, while the underlying concepts of UNIX are explained in depth.

Life with UNIX: A Guide for Everyone. Don Libes and Sandy Ressler, Prentice Hall, 1989. A witty guide to UNIX, more interesting for its account of UNIX's development over the years. It's a little hard to find, but worth the effort.

UNIX System V Release 4: An Introduction for New and Experienced Users. Kenneth Rosen, Richard Rosinski, and James Farber, Osborne McGraw-Hill, 1990. This 1,200-page guide to UNIX is the most thorough documentation of SVR4 in one volume.

UNIX in a Nutshell. Daniel Gilly, O'Reilly & Associates, 1992. More than you ever wanted to learn about UNIX commands.

Learning the UNIX Operating System. Grace Todino, John Strang, and Jerry Peek, O'Reilly & Associates, 1993.

Text Editing and Processing

Text Processing and Typesetting With UNIX. David Barron and Mike Rees,

Addison-Wesley, 1987.

Troff Typesetting for UNIX Systems. Sandra Emersom and Karen Paulsell,

Prentice Hall, 1987.

The Ultimate Guide to the vi and ex Text Editors. Hewlett-Packard Co., Benjamin Cummings, 1990.

Linux Titles

Linux in Plain English. Patrick Volkerding and Kevin Reichard, MIS:Press, 1997. This book covers the Linux command set in some detail, although in the same general fashion as UNIX in Plain English.

Linux Configuration and Installation, third edition. Patrick Volkerding, Kevin Reichard,and Eric Foster-Johnson, MIS:Press, 1997. This book covers the installation and configuration of Linux. Slackware Linux is included on an accompanying CD-ROM.

INDEX

A

apropos, 44
ar, 364
at, 376-378
atq, 379
atrm, 380
awk, 162

B

banner, 196
basename, 45
batch, 381
bc, 46-48
bdftopcf, 238
bdiff, 102
bitmap, 239-240

C

cal, 49
calendar, 50-51
cancel, 197
calctool, 241

D

E

F

G

H

I

J

join, 132-133

K

kill, 74
ksh, 75

L

listusers, 76
ln, 134-135
login, 386
logname, 212
lp, 198-199
lpsched, 201
lpshut, 200
lpstat, 202-203
ls, 136-138

M

mailtool, 275-276
mailx, 213-214
make, 370-371
man, 77
mesg, 215